FOREWORD

It has been 25 years since the first Special 301 Report was published in 1989. The first report, called a "Fact Sheet," highlighted 25 trading partners – eight on the Priority Watch List and 17 on the Watch List.

Over the past 25 years, the Special 301 Report has identified positive advances as well as areas of continued concern. The Report has reflected changing technologies, promoted best practices, and situated these critical issues in their policy context, underscoring the importance of intellectual property rights protection and enforcement to the United States and our trading partners.

During this period, there has been significant progress in a variety of countries. For instance, Korea, which appeared on the Priority Watch List in the original 1989 Fact Sheet, has since been removed from both the Priority Watch List and the Watch List. Korea has transformed itself from a country in need of intellectual property rights enforcement into a country with a reputation for cutting-edge innovation as well as high-quality, high-tech manufacturing. Korea is now one of the top patent filers internationally and a U.S. trade agreement partner with state-of-the art standards of intellectual property rights protection and enforcement. Italy, which was first placed on the Watch List in 1989, is removed from the Watch List in 2014 in recognition of its latest effort, addressing copyright piracy over the Internet. Likewise, the Philippines, which was first placed on the Watch List in 1989, is removed from the Watch List in 2014 based on sustained actions that the Philippine government has undertaken to improve intellectual property rights protection and civil and administrative enforcement in the Philippines. There have also been important advances in many other markets over the past 25 years that have been reflected in the Special 301 Report, including in Australia, Israel, Japan, Qatar, Spain, Taiwan, the United Arab Emirates, and Uruguay.

Still, considerable concerns remain. In 2014, 10 countries are on the Priority Watch List and 27 countries are on the Watch List. Several countries, including Chile, China, India, Indonesia, Thailand, and Turkey, have been listed every year since the Report's inception.

The Special 301 Report serves a critical function by identifying opportunities and challenges facing our innovative and creative industries in foreign markets and by promoting the job creation, economic development, and many other benefits that effective intellectual property protection and enforcement support. The Special 301 Report informs the public and our trading partners and can serve as a positive catalyst for change. USTR remains committed to meaningful and sustained engagement with our trading partners, with the goal of resolving these challenges.

ACKNOWLEDGEMENTS

The Office of the United States Trade Representative (USTR) is responsible for the preparation of this Report. United States Trade Representative Michael Froman gratefully acknowledges the contributions of all USTR staff to the writing and production of this Report. USTR extends its thanks to partner agencies, including the Departments of State, the Treasury, Justice, Agriculture, Commerce, Labor, Health and Human Services, and Homeland Security, and the U.S. Copyright Office.

In preparing the Report, substantial information was solicited from U.S. Embassies around the world, from U.S. Government agencies, and from interested stakeholders. The draft of this Report was developed through the Special 301 Subcommittee of the interagency Trade Policy Staff Committee.

April 2014

TABLE OF CONTENTS

EXECUTIVE SUMMARY

The Special 301 Report is the result of an annual review of the state of intellectual property rights (IPR) protection and enforcement in U.S. trading partners around world, which the Office of the United States Trade Representative (USTR) conducts pursuant to Section 182 of the Trade Act of 1974, as amended by the Omnibus Trade and Competitiveness Act of 1988 and the Uruguay Round Agreements Act (19 U.S.C. § 2242).

This Report reflects the Administration's continued resolve to encourage and maintain adequate and effective IPR protection and enforcement worldwide. It identifies a wide range of concerns, including: (a) the deterioration in IPR protection, enforcement, and market access for persons relying on IPR in a number of trading partners; (b) reported inadequacies in trade secret protection in China, India, and elsewhere, as well as an increasing incidence of trade secret misappropriation; (c) troubling "indigenous innovation" policies that may unfairly disadvantage U.S. rights holders in China; (d) the continuing challenges of copyright piracy over the Internet in countries such as Brazil, China, India, and Russia; (e) market access barriers, including nontransparent, discriminatory or otherwise trade-restrictive measures, that appear to impede access to healthcare; and (f) other ongoing, systemic IPR enforcement issues in many trading partners around the world.

USTR looks forward to working closely with the governments of the trading partners that are identified in this year's Special 301 Report, to address both emerging and continuing concerns, and to continue to build on the positive results that many of these governments have achieved.

Public Engagement

USTR continued to enhance public engagement in this year's Special 301 process, to facilitate sound, well-balanced assessments of IPR protection and enforcement efforts of particular trading partners, and to help ensure that the Special 301 review is based on a full understanding of the various IPR issues in trading partner markets. USTR requested written submissions from the public through a notice published in the *Federal Register* on January 3, 2014. In addition, on February 24, USTR conducted a public hearing that provided the opportunity for interested persons to testify before the interagency Special 301 Subcommittee about issues relevant to the review. The hearing featured testimony from witnesses such as representatives of foreign governments, industry, and non-governmental organizations. For the first time, USTR recorded and posted on its website the testimony at the Special 301 hearing, and also offered a two-week post-hearing comment period during which hearing participants and interested parties could submit additional information in support of, or in response to, hearing testimony. The 2014 *Federal Register* notice – and post-hearing comment period – drew submissions from over 100 interested parties, including 21 trading partner governments. These submissions are available to the public online at www.regulations.gov, docket number USTR-2013-0040. The public can access both the video and transcript of the hearing at www.ustr.gov.

Country Placement

The Special 301 designations and actions announced in this Report are the result of deliberations among all relevant agencies within the U.S. Government, informed by extensive consultation with affected stakeholders, foreign governments, the U.S. Congress, and other interested parties.

USTR, together with the Special 301 Subcommittee of the Trade Policy Staff Committee, conducts a balanced assessment of U.S. trading partners' IPR protection and enforcement, as well as related market access issues, in accordance with the statutory criteria set out by the U.S. Congress. (*See* Annex I).

This assessment is necessarily conducted on a case-by-case basis, taking into account diverse factors such as a trading partner's level of development, its international obligations and commitments, the concerns of rights holders and other interested parties, and the trade and investment policies of the United States. It is informed by the various cross-cutting issues and trends identified below in *Section I – Developments in Intellectual Property Rights Protection and Enforcement*. Each assessment is based upon the specific facts and circumstances that shape IPR protection and enforcement regimes in a particular trading partner.

In the year ahead, USTR will continue its bilateral engagement with the governments of the trading partners that are discussed in this Report. In preparation for, and in the course of, those interactions, USTR will:

- Engage with U.S. stakeholders, the U.S. Congress, and other interested parties to ensure that the U.S. Government's position is well-informed by the full range of views on the pertinent issues;

- Conduct extensive discussions with individual trading partners regarding their respective IPR regimes;

- Encourage those trading partners to engage fully, and with the greatest degree of transparency, with the full range of stakeholders on IPR matters; and

- Identify, where possible, appropriate ways in which the U.S. Government can be of assistance. (*See* Annex 2 for examples).

USTR will conduct these discussions in a manner that both advances the policy goals of the United States and respects the importance of meaningful policy dialogue with U.S. trading partners. Additionally, USTR will continue to work closely with other U.S. Government agencies to ensure consistency of U.S. trade policy objectives with other Administration policies.

2014 Special 301 List

The Special 301 Subcommittee of the TPSC reviewed 82 trading partners in this year's Special 301 process. The Subcommittee received stakeholder input on nearly 100 trading partners, but focused the review on those submissions that complied with the requirement in the *Federal*

Register notice to identify whether a particular trading partner should be named as a Priority Foreign Country (PFC), placed on the Priority Watch List (PWL) or Watch List (WL), or not listed in the Report, and that were received by the deadlines provided in the notice. Following extensive research and analysis, USTR has listed 37 trading partners as follows:

> <u>Priority Watch List</u>: Algeria; Argentina; Chile; China; India; Indonesia; Pakistan; Russia; Thailand; and Venezuela; and

> <u>Watch List</u>: Barbados; Belarus; Bolivia; Brazil; Bulgaria; Canada; Colombia; Costa Rica; Dominican Republic; Ecuador; Egypt; Finland; Greece; Guatemala; Jamaica; Kuwait; Lebanon; Mexico; Paraguay; Peru; Romania; Tajikistan; Trinidad and Tobago; Turkey; Turkmenistan; Uzbekistan; and Vietnam.

The Report also provides an update on the results of the Section 301 investigation of Ukraine following Ukraine's designation as a Priority Foreign Country on May 1, 2013.

Out-of-Cycle Reviews

An Out-of-Cycle Review (OCR) is a tool that USTR uses to encourage progress on IPR issues of concern. It provides an opportunity for heightened engagement and cooperation with trading partners to address and remedy such issues. Successful resolution of specific IPR issues of concern can also lead to a change in a trading partner's Special 301 status outside of the typical time frame for the annual Special 301 Report. In the coming months, USTR will conduct OCRs of Priority Watch List country India and Watch List countries Kuwait and Paraguay. Details appear in the country-specific discussions below. Although Spain is not listed in the 2014 Special 301 Report, USTR will continue to conduct an OCR of Spain, announced in 2013, that is focused in particular on concrete steps taken by Spain to combat copyright piracy over the Internet. USTR may conduct additional OCRs of other trading partners as circumstances warrant, or as requested by the trading partner.

Out-of-Cycle Review of Notorious Markets

In 2010, USTR began publishing the Notorious Markets List as an OCR separately from the annual Special 301 Report. The Notorious Markets List identifies selected markets, including online markets, that are reportedly engaged in piracy and counterfeiting, according to information submitted to USTR in response to a request for comments pursuant to a *Federal Register* notice. USTR requested such comments on September 20, 2013, and published the 2013 Notorious Markets List on February 12, 2014. USTR plans to conduct its next Notorious Markets OCR in the fall of 2014. The Notorious Markets List is available at <u>www.ustr.gov</u>.

Format of the Special 301 Report

The Special 301 Report is divided into the following two Sections and three Annexes.

- **Section I. Developments in Intellectual Property Rights Protection and Enforcement** discusses broad global trends and issues in IPR protection and enforcement that the U.S. Government works to address on a daily basis.

- **Section II. Country Reports** includes descriptions of issues of concern with respect to particular trading partners.

- **Annex 1** describes the statutory basis of the Special 301 Report.

- **Annex 2** highlights U. S. Government-sponsored technical assistance and capacity building efforts.

- **Annex 3** highlights new ratifications and accessions to the World Intellectual Property Organization (WIPO) Performances and Phonograms Treaty (WPPT) and the WIPO Copyright Treaty (WCT) (collectively, the WIPO Internet Treaties).

SECTION I. DEVELOPMENTS IN INTELLECTUAL PROPERTY RIGHTS PROTECTION AND ENFORCEMENT

An important part of the mission of USTR is to support and implement the Administration's commitment to protect vigorously the interests of U.S. holders of intellectual property rights overseas while preserving the incentives that ensure access to and widespread dissemination of the fruits of innovation and creativity. IPR infringement, including trademark counterfeiting and copyright piracy, causes significant financial losses for rights holders and legitimate businesses around the world. It undermines key U.S. comparative advantages in innovation and creativity, to the detriment of American businesses and workers. In its most pernicious forms, IPR infringement endangers the public. Some counterfeit products, such as semiconductors, automobile parts, and medicines, pose significant risks to consumer health and safety. In addition, trade in counterfeit and pirated products often fuels cross-border organized criminal networks and hinders the sustainable economic development of many countries.

Because fostering innovation and creativity is essential to U.S. prosperity, competitiveness, and the support of an estimated 40 million U.S. jobs that directly or indirectly rely on intellectual property-intensive industries, USTR works to protect American innovation and creativity with all the tools of U.S. trade policy, including this Report.

Positive Developments

The United States welcomes the following important steps by our trading partners in 2013 and early 2014.

- **Algeria** – In October 2013, Algeria submitted its instrument of accession to the WIPO Internet Treaties. Adopted in Geneva in December 1996, the treaties are designed to maintain the protection of the rights of authors, performers, and producers of phonograms in the digital age. The treaties entered into force for Algeria on January 31, 2014.

- **China** – In August 2013, the National People's Congress enacted important amendments to China's Trademark Law, including provisions to combat trademark squatting, expand protection to sound marks, permit multi-class registration, and streamline application and appeal procedures. The United States welcomes these long-sought reforms, but notes that a number of important issues not clarified in the law need to be addressed in implementing regulations that are still under development. The United States will continue to work closely with China to address these concerns as the implementing regulations are drafted, adopted, and enter into force. The United States also looks forward to pending reforms of China's patent, copyright, trade secrets, and other IP-related laws and regulations.

- **European Union (EU)** – On November 28, 2013, the European Commission introduced a proposal for a Directive of the European Parliament and of the Council on the

Protection of Undisclosed Know-How and Business Information (Trade Secrets) Against Their Unlawful Acquisition, Use and Disclosure. This Directive would harmonize civil trade secret law throughout the EU. The United States welcomes this important step and looks forward to continued progress on this draft measure specifically, and on EU efforts to protect trade secrets from theft and misappropriation generally.

- **Israel** – On January 23, 2014, Israel passed patent legislation that satisfied its remaining commitments under a 2010 Memorandum of Understanding (MOU) with the United States. As a result of the successful execution of the MOU, Israel has taken legal and regulatory measures to make its patent system more transparent, efficient, and effective, and was removed from the Watch List earlier this year.

- **Italy** – Italy is removed from the Watch List in the 2014 Special 301 Report in recognition of the Italian Communications Regulatory Authority's (AGCOM) adoption, on December 12, 2013, of long-awaited regulations to combat copyright piracy over the Internet. The regulations, which entered into force on March 31, 2014, provide notice-and-takedown procedures that incorporate due process safeguards and establish a mechanism for addressing large-scale piracy. The adoption and entry into force of these regulations is a significant achievement, resulting from intensive efforts over many years, which the United States strongly welcomes. We look forward to continuing to work with Italy on our shared commitment to IPR protection and enforcement, and will closely monitor Italy's implementation of these regulations.

- **Paraguay** – On October 10, 2013, President Cartes signed the implementing regulation (Decree 460) for Law 4798 of 2012 that created the National Directorate of Intellectual Property (DINAPI). DINAPI is now the Paraguayan government authority responsible for the administration of copyrights, trademarks, patents, industrial designs, and geographic indications. Additionally, the law authorizes DINAPI's enforcement arm, the General Enforcement Directorate, to conduct administrative investigations and initiate proceedings at customs checkpoints and businesses.

- **Philippines** – The Philippines is removed from the Watch List in the 2014 Special 301 Report. This decision was based on the collective weight of a series of significant legislative reforms, a move toward more effective civil and administrative enforcement efforts, IP authorities' sustained and constructive engagement with the U.S. Government and members of the private sector, and commitments to continue to address remaining concerns.

The United States will continue to work with its trading partners to further enhance IPR protection and enforcement during the coming year.

Best IPR Practices by Trading Partners

USTR highlights the following best practices by trading partners in the area of IPR protection and enforcement.

- USTR continues to encourage trading partners to work with the United States to develop action plans to advance the protection and enforcement of IPR. USTR welcomes the offer of the Government of Bulgaria to develop an action plan, and is working with a number of other trading partners, including the Government of Pakistan, to develop action plans to address the issues discussed in the Special 301 Report. USTR looks forward to continuing to work with these trading partners to finalize and implement these action plans as well as to work with other trading partners on implementing existing action plans.

- USTR supports transparency and meaningful stakeholder participation in the development of laws, regulations, procedures, and other measures as well as meaningful engagement between governments and stakeholders. Stakeholders report that such transparency and participation allows governments to avoid unintended consequences and makes it easier for stakeholders to comply with legislative or regulatory changes once adopted and implemented.

- Cooperation among different government agencies is another example of a best practice. Several countries, including the United States, have introduced IPR enforcement coordination mechanisms or agreements to enhance interagency cooperation. In Paraguay, DINAPI, operational since October 2013, has signed several inter-institutional agreements to enhance cooperation on IPR, including with Paraguayan enforcement agencies that have jurisdiction over customs and other IP-related violations. In Algeria, the National Office of Intellectual Property Rights (ONDA) signed cooperation agreements with Algerian customs and other Algerian law enforcement entities on training and operational coordination to strengthen efforts to interdict illicit goods. The Philippines' National IPR Committee, led by that country's Intellectual Property Office, provides another example of enhanced interagency cooperation. The United States encourages other trading partners to consider adopting similar cooperative IPR arrangements.

- Several trading partners have participated or supported participation in innovative mechanisms that enable government and private sector rights holders to voluntarily donate or license IPR on mutually agreed terms and conditions. In these arrangements, parties use existing IPR to advance innovation and public policy goals. The United

12

States was the first government in the world to share its patents with the Medicines Patent Pool, an independent foundation hosted by the World Health Organization (WHO). The United States hopes that additional public and private patent holders will explore voluntary licenses with the Medicines Patent Pool as one of many innovative ways to help improve the availability of medicines in developing countries. The patents that the United States shared were related to protease inhibitor medicines, primarily used to treat drug-resistant HIV infections. In addition, the United States, Brazil, and South Africa are providers in the WIPO *Re:Search* Consortium, a voluntary mechanism for making IPR and know how available on mutually agreed terms and conditions to the global health research community to find cures or treatments for neglected tropical diseases, and for malaria and tuberculosis. Other countries have joined as supporters.

- Finally, another best practice is the active participation of government officials in capacity building efforts and in training. As further explained in Annex 2, the United States encourages foreign governments to make training opportunities available to their officials, and it actively engages with its trading partners in capacity building efforts both in the United States and abroad.

Initiatives to Strengthen IPR Protection and Enforcement Internationally

The United States works to promote adequate and effective protection and enforcement of IPR through the following mechanisms.

- **Trans-Pacific Partnership (TPP):** The Trans-Pacific Partnership is a key initiative through which the United States seeks to advance multifaceted U.S. trade and investment interests in the Asia-Pacific region by negotiating an ambitious, 21st-century regional trade agreement along with Australia, Brunei Darussalam, Canada, Chile, Malaysia, Mexico, New Zealand, Peru, Singapore, and Vietnam, in addition to Japan, which joined negotiations in 2013. The TPP negotiations are being undertaken with this group of like-minded countries with the goal of creating a platform for integration across the region, including strong standards for the protection and enforcement of IPR and for addressing emerging issues in the 21st century.

- **Transatlantic Trade and Investment Partnership (T-TIP):** On March 20, 2013, the USTR notified the U.S. Congress of the President's intent to enter into negotiations for a comprehensive trade and investment agreement with the EU. Since that notification, the United States and the EU have held four rounds of negotiations, most recently during the week of March 10, 2014. With respect to IPR, the United States and the EU provide among the highest levels of IPR protection and the most robust IPR enforcement in the world. In T-TIP, the United States is pursuing a targeted approach on IPR that will reflect the shared U.S.-EU objective of high-level IPR protection and enforcement, and sustained and enhanced joint leadership on IPR issues. The United States will seek new opportunities to advance and defend the interests of U.S. creators, innovators, businesses, farmers, and workers with respect to strong protection and effective enforcement of IPR, including their ability to compete in foreign markets.

- **World Trade Organization (WTO):** The multilateral structure of the WTO provides opportunities for USTR to lead engagement with trading partners on IPR issues in several contexts, including through accession negotiations for prospective Members, the Council for Trade-Related Aspects of Intellectual Property Rights (TRIPS Council), and the Dispute Settlement Body. In the past year, the United States sponsored discussions in the TRIPS Council on the positive role of IPR protection and enforcement in contributing to national innovation environments, including with respect to low-cost innovation and social entrepreneurship, and university research and technology transfer partnerships. These discussions, which involved contributions from a broad array of WTO Members, including developed, developing, and least-developed countries, addressed national IP strategies to promote innovation, focusing in particular on the role IP plays in driving critical financing, commercialization, and partnerships to bring ideas to market. The United States has also actively engaged in TRIPS Council discussions on the positive role of IP in promoting climate technology innovation and transfer. These discussions highlighted the global nature of climate technology innovation and the beneficial contributions of IPR protection and enforcement on technology innovation and transfer. Additionally, the United States co-sponsored discussions on IP and sports, with broad engagement from numerous and diverse WTO Members, focusing on the critical relationship between sports (including major sporting events such as the Olympics, World Cup, and national leagues) and IP (including copyright for broadcasting content, patents and trade secrets for cutting-edge sports equipment, and trademarks for branding and sponsorship).

- **Bilateral and Regional Initiatives:** The United States works with many trading partners to strengthen IPR protection and enforcement through the provisions of bilateral and regional agreements, including trade agreements). In addition, Trade and Investment Framework Agreements (TIFAs) between the United States and numerous trading partners around the world have facilitated discussions on enhancing IPR protection and enforcement.

- **Anti-Counterfeiting Trade Agreement (ACTA):** On October 5, 2012, Japan became the first signatory to ACTA to deposit its instrument of acceptance. The United States continues to work with Japan and other negotiating parties to bring the ACTA into force. The ACTA effort, launched in October 2007, brought together a number of like-minded countries prepared to embrace strengthened IPR enforcement and cooperative enforcement practices. ACTA signatories are Australia, Canada, Japan, South Korea, Mexico, Morocco, New Zealand, Singapore, and the United States. The European Union and 22 EU Member States signed the Agreement in January 2012, but it was not approved by the European Parliament. For signatories, the next step towards bringing the ACTA into force is to deposit instruments of ratification, acceptance, or approval. The ACTA will enter into force for those signatories 30 days following the deposit of the sixth such instrument. The ACTA includes innovative provisions to deepen international cooperation and to promote strong enforcement practices, and will ultimately help sustain American jobs in innovative and creative industries.

- **Trade Preference Program Reviews:** USTR, in coordination with other agencies, reviews IPR practices in connection with the implementation of trade preference programs, such as the Generalized System of Preferences (GSP) program, and regional programs, including the Caribbean Basin Economic Recovery Act and the Caribbean Basin Trade Partnership Act.

- **Enhanced International Cooperation:** USTR, in coordination with other U.S. Government agencies, looks forward to continuing engagement with trading partners in bilateral, regional, and multilateral fora to improve the global IPR environment. In addition to the work described above, the United States anticipates engaging with its trading partners on IPR-related initiatives in multilateral and regional fora such as the U.S.-EU Summit, G-8, Asia-Pacific Economic Cooperation (APEC), World Intellectual Property Organization (WIPO), and Organization for Economic Cooperation and Development (OECD).

Trade Secrets and Forced Technology Transfer

International and foreign market issues

The Special 301 Report again reflects an emphasis on the need to protect and enforce trade secrets. Companies in a wide variety of industry sectors – including information and communication technologies, services, biopharmaceuticals, manufacturing, and environmental technologies – rely on the ability to protect and enforce their trade secrets and rights in other proprietary information. Indeed, trade secrets are often among a company's core business assets, and a company's competitiveness may depend on its capacity to protect such assets.

Trade secret theft, including industrial and economic espionage, which imposes significant costs on U.S. companies and threatens the security of the United States, appears to be escalating. If a company's trade secrets are stolen, it may be extremely difficult, if not impossible, to recoup past investments in research and development, and future innovation may be compromised. Moreover, trade secret theft threatens to diminish U.S. competitiveness around the globe, and puts American jobs at risk. The reach of trade secret theft into critical commercial and defense technologies poses threats to U.S. national security interests as well.

For these reasons, the United States is concerned by gaps in trade secret protection and enforcement, and the apparent growth of trade secret theft, particularly in China, as reported by various sources, including the Office of the National Counterintelligence Executive (ONCIX). The ONCIX publication titled *Foreign Spies Stealing U.S. Economic Secrets in Cyberspace*, states that "Chinese actors are the world's most active and persistent perpetrators of economic espionage." Theft may arise in a variety of circumstances, including those involving departing employees, failed joint ventures, cyber intrusion and hacking, and misuse of information submitted to government entities for purposes of complying with regulatory obligations. In practice, effective remedies, including under Chinese law, appear to be difficult to obtain.

The United States urges its trading partners to ensure that they have robust systems for protecting and enforcing trade secrets, including the availability of deterrent criminal penalties for trade secret theft. USTR will monitor developments in this area.

U.S. Government strategy

On February 20, 2013, the U.S. Intellectual Property Enforcement Coordinator (IPEC) issued the *Administration Strategy on Mitigating the Theft of U.S. Trade Secrets*. The Strategy highlights U.S. efforts to combat the theft of trade secrets that could be used by foreign governments or companies to gain an unfair economic advantage by harming U.S. innovation and creativity, including:

- Focusing diplomatic efforts to protect trade secrets overseas, which include sustained and coordinated engagement with trading partners, the use of trade policy tools (including through the use of the Special 301 Report), cooperation, and training, among others;

- Promoting voluntary best practices by private industry to protect trade secrets, including information security, physical security, and human resources policies;

- Enhancing domestic law enforcement operations, especially through the activities of the Department of Justice, Federal Bureau of Investigations, Department of Defense, and the National IPR Coordination Center;

- Improving domestic legislation to protect against trade secret theft, as exemplified by the *Theft of Trade Secrets Clarification Act of 2012*, which clarified provisions in the *Economic Espionage Act* with respect to the theft of trade secret source codes, and the *Foreign and Economic Espionage Penalty Enhancement Act of 2012*, which increased criminal penalties for economic espionage; and

- Conducting public awareness campaigns and stakeholder outreach to encourage all stakeholders to be aware of the dangers of trade secret theft.

Trade secret theft can be viewed as a form of forced technology transfer that foreign actors may use to undermine U.S. competitive advantage. Foreign governments may also adopt trade-distortive policies, which are sometimes designed to promote "indigenous innovation" by forcing U.S. companies to transfer their technology or other valuable commercial information. Examples of these policies, include, but are not limited to:

- Requiring the transfer of technology as a condition for obtaining regulatory approvals or otherwise securing access to a market, or for allowing a company to continue to do business in the market;

- Directing state-owned enterprises in innovative sectors to seek non-commercial terms from their foreign business partners, including with respect to the acquisition and use or licensing of IPR;

- Failing to effectively enforce IPR, including patents, trademarks, trade secrets, and copyrights, thereby allowing national firms to gain a competitive advantage over their foreign competitors through misappropriation or infringement of the competitor's IPR;

- Failing to take meaningful measures to prevent or deter cyber intrusions and other unauthorized activities;

- Requiring use of, or providing preferences to, products or services in which IPR is either developed or owned locally, including with respect to government procurement;

- Manipulating the standards development process to create unfair advantages for national firms, including with respect to the terms on which IPR is licensed; and

- Requiring the submission of excessive (and often unnecessary) confidential business information for regulatory approval purposes, and failing to appropriately protect such information from unfair commercial use by, and disclosure to, third parties.

The United States urges that, in formulating policies to promote innovation, trading partners, including India and China, take account of the increasingly cross-border nature of commercial research and development, and of the importance of voluntary and mutually agreed commercial partnerships.

Intellectual Property and the Environment

Strong IPR protection is vital for development, and is critical to responding to environmental challenges, including climate change. IPR protection is essential to facilitate access to today's technologies, and to promote tomorrow's innovation. IPR provides incentives to invest in green technologies, and can promote economic growth and create jobs in the green technology sector. Without such incentives, businesses are reluctant to invest or enter into technology transfer arrangements in countries that lack effective IPR protection and enforcement. IPR is also an important driver of university research in the green technology sector. In the absence of such technologies, society may be deprived of critical advances to meet environmental challenges, including the mitigation of, and adaptation to, climate change.

Certain national policies and practices advanced domestically and in multilateral fora may have the unintended effect of undermining national and global efforts to address serious environmental challenges. For example, India's National Manufacturing Policy promotes the compulsory licensing of patented technologies as a means of effectuating technology transfer with respect to green technologies. India has pressed to multilateralize this approach to green technologies through its proposals in the negotiations under the United Nations Framework Convention on Climate Change (UNFCCC). These actions will discourage rather than promote the investment in, and dissemination of, green technologies, including those technologies that contribute to climate change adaptation and mitigation.

The United States continues to work to ensure robust IP protection and enforcement, which gives inventors and creators the confidence to: engage in foreign direct investment, joint ventures, local partnerships, and licensing arrangements; collaborate with foreign counterparts; to open research facilities in markets abroad; establish local operations and work with local manufacturers and suppliers; create jobs, including local worker training; and invest in infrastructure for the production, adoption, and delivery of green technology goods and services, without fear of misappropriation of their IPR. Strong IPR protection is, therefore, not only critical to the objective of addressing environmental challenges and developing a global response to climate change, but to national economic growth. The United States promotes strong IPR protection and enforcement as an environmental as well as an economic imperative, providing critical developmental benefits for developing and least-developed countries in particular.

Trends in Trademark Counterfeiting and Copyright Piracy

The problems of trademark counterfeiting and copyright piracy continue on a global scale and involve mass production and sales of a vast array of fake goods, including counterfeit semiconductors, medicines, health care products, food and beverages, automobile parts, such as air bags, aircraft parts, apparel and footwear, toothpaste, toys, shampoos, razors, electronics, batteries, chemicals, sporting goods, motion pictures, and music.

Consumers, legitimate producers, and governments are harmed by rampant trademark counterfeiting and copyright piracy. Consumers may be harmed by fraudulent and potentially dangerous counterfeit products, including medicines, auto and airplane parts, and semiconductors. Producers face the risk of diminished profits and loss of reputation when consumers purchase fake products, and governments may lose tax revenue and find it more difficult to attract investment. Infringers generally pay no taxes or duties, and often disregard basic standards for worker health and safety and product quality and performance.

An example illustrating the extent of the economic harm arising from such trademark counterfeiting and copyright piracy comes from India. In September 2013, the International Chamber of Commerce and the Federation of Indian Chambers of Commerce and Industry published a study analyzing seven key industry sectors vulnerable to counterfeiting, piracy, and smuggling, *e.g.*, automotive parts, alcohol, computer hardware, mobile phones, packaged foods, personal goods, and tobacco products. The study concluded that rights holders in 2012 suffered lost sales in India amounting to 21.7 percent or approximately $11.9 billion due to these problems. Collectively, the Indian government's economic loss tied to these illicit activities totaled approximately $4.26 billion, according to the study.

Industry reports trends in counterfeiting and piracy that include:

- Sustained growth in the piracy of copyrighted products in virtually all formats as well as counterfeiting of trademarked goods. The involvement of criminal enterprises continues to rise, often because piracy and counterfeiting offer enormous profits and little risk. Such enterprises require little up-front capital investment, and even when they are detected and prosecuted, the penalties imposed on them in many countries are very low and therefore offer little or no deterrence against further infringements. Instead, the penalties are viewed merely as a cost of doing business;

- Continued growth in the online sale of pirated and counterfeit hard goods that will soon surpass the volume of such goods sold by street vendors and in other physical markets. Enforcement authorities, unfortunately, face difficulties in responding to this trend. Online advertisements for the sale of illicit physical goods that are delivered through express mail shipments or by small consignments are found in many places;

- A continued increase in the use of legitimate services to deliver infringing goods, making it more difficult for enforcement officials to detect these goods;

- An increase in the practice of shipping counterfeit products separately from labels and packaging in order to evade enforcement efforts; and

- The emergence of Media Box piracy, whereby those boxes, often with capability to play high definition content, are loaded with large quantities of pirated works or are configured to facilitate the user's access to websites featuring unlicensed content. This problem has been reported in China (including Hong Kong), Indonesia, Malaysia, Taiwan, Thailand, and Vietnam.

The United States continues to urge trading partners to undertake more effective criminal and border enforcement to stop the manufacture, import, export, transit, and distribution of pirated and counterfeit goods. USTR engages extensively with its trading partners through bilateral consultations, trade agreements, and international organizations, to ensure that penalties are deterrent, and include significant monetary fines and meaningful sentences of imprisonment. Additionally, important elements of a deterrent enforcement system include requirements that pirated and counterfeit goods, as well as the materials and implements used for their production, be seized and destroyed, rather than being re-exported or otherwise allowed to reenter the channels of commerce. Such re-export or entrance into the channels of commerce creates IPR enforcement problems and potential health and safety risks for other trading partners or for the original country of importation. Providing enforcement officials with the authority to seize suspect counterfeit trademark or pirated copyright goods during their import or export, or in transit movement, without the need for a formal complaint from a rights holder is also critical to effective enforcement. The U.S. Government supports trading partners through technical assistance and sharing of best practices on enforcement, including destruction of seized goods. (*See* Annex 2).

The manufacture and distribution of pharmaceutical products bearing counterfeit trademarks is a growing problem that has important consequences for consumer health and safety. Such trademark counterfeiting is one dimension of the larger problem of substandard medicines. The United States notes its particular concern with the proliferation of counterfeit pharmaceuticals manufactured, sold and distributed in trading partners such as Brazil, China, Indonesia, Lebanon, Peru, Russia, and especially in India, the largest source of counterfeit pharmaceuticals shipped to the United States. Reports indicate that anywhere from 10-40 percent of drugs sold in Indian markets are counterfeit and could represent a serious threat to patient health and safety. The U.S. Government, through the United States Agency for International Development, and other agencies, supports programs in Sub-Saharan Africa and elsewhere that assist trading partners in protecting the public against counterfeit medicines introduced into their markets.

In many cases, the bulk active pharmaceutical ingredients (API) that are used to manufacture pharmaceuticals that bear counterfeit trademarks are not made according to good manufacturing practices. Hence, these products may contain sub-standard and potentially hazardous materials. For instance, in China, some domestic chemical manufacturers that produce API have avoided regulatory oversight by failing to declare that bulk chemicals are intended for use in pharmaceutical products. This contributes to China being a major source country for APIs used in counterfeit pharmaceutical products. Although China has taken some welcome steps, such as requiring manufacturers to register with the State Food and Drug Administration, more effective regulatory controls are needed.

Digital, Internet, and Broadcast Piracy

The increased availability of broadband Internet connections around the world is generating many benefits, from increased economic activity and new business models to greater access to and exchange of information. However, this phenomenon has also made the Internet an extremely efficient vehicle for disseminating copyright-infringing products, supplanting legitimate opportunities for rights holders. The U.S. Government's 2013 Notorious Markets List includes examples of online marketplaces reportedly engaging in commercial-scale IPR infringement, including sites hosted in or operated by parties located in Canada, China, the Netherlands, Russia, Sweden, Ukraine, and elsewhere.

Piracy over the Internet is a significant concern in many U.S. trading partners. Unauthorized retransmission of live sports telecasts over the Internet continues to be a growing problem for many trading partners, particularly China, and websites that link to infringing content are exacerbating the problem.

U.S. copyright industries also report growing problems with piracy using mobile telephones, tablets, flash drives, and other mobile technologies. In some countries, these devices are pre-loaded with illegal content even before they are sold.

In addition to piracy of music and films, U.S. industry reports the emergence of pirate servers, or "grey shards." Players of cloud-based entertainment software access these unauthorized servers to play copyrighted games that are made available through hacked software or circumvention of technological protection measures, which are used by rights holders to control unauthorized access to, and prevent unauthorized copying of, protected content.

The problem of online piracy is exacerbated due to the development and sale of devices that allow for the circumvention of technological protection measures (TPM). Such devices include "game copiers" and mod chips that make it possible to play pirated games on gaming systems. Software that enables TPM circumvention is also distributed online. For example, SlySoft, a company headquartered and operating in Antigua, developed and sells a program called "Any DVD HD" that enables the user to defeat the encryption technology embedded in Blu-ray Discs that prevents unauthorized reproduction and distribution. Antigua's Copyright Act makes it illegal to manufacture or import for sale or rental any such circumvention device. The consortium of electronic manufacturers, software companies, and motion picture studios that developed these technological protection measures has worked with the criminal enforcement authorities in Antigua for over seven years to enforce this statute and have this case prosecuted. In April 2014, the owner and operator of Slysoft was found guilty of providing tools to circumvent encryption and was fined $30,000. It is unclear whether the Government of Antigua and Barbuda will permit the site to continue operating now that its courts have determined the conduct to be unlawful. The United States will continue to monitor the situation.

The United States continues to have serious concerns regarding Switzerland's system of online copyright protection and enforcement. The United States strongly encourages Switzerland to demonstrate its commitment to copyright protection and to combating online piracy by taking steps to ensure that rights holders can protect their rights. The United States welcomes many aspects of the December 2013 report of the AGUR 12 working group on copyright and urges the Swiss government to move forward expeditiously with measures to appropriately and effectively address copyright piracy in Switzerland. The United States looks forward to working with Swiss authorities in their heightened engagement with respect to this priority issue.

The United States also encourages trading partners to adopt appropriate measures where needed to address the unauthorized camcording of motion pictures in theaters. The effects of this conduct are not always limited to the market in which this unauthorized recording occurs. For example, as discussed in more detail below, according to the Motion Pictures Distributors Association of India, India has one of the highest rates of piracy of audiovisual works in the world, and in 2012, the motion picture industry experienced losses estimated at $1.1 billion, an increase of 15.79 percent from 2008.

Copies of copyright-protected material, including audiovisual works that have been camcorded, are often distributed without authorization over the Internet. The United States encourages trading partners to enhance enforcement efforts against this form of infringement by: establishing deterrent penalties against camcording; strengthening enforcement against major channels of piracy over the Internet, including with respect to notorious markets; and creating specialized, trained enforcement units and undertaking special initiatives against Internet piracy.

Although copyright piracy over the Internet is rapidly supplanting physical piracy in many markets around the world, the production of, and trade in, pirated optical discs remains a major problems in many regions. In recent years, some trading partners, such as the Czech Republic, Poland, Romania, and Russia, have made progress toward implementing controls on optical media production. Other trading partners still need to adopt and implement legislation or improve existing measures to combat illegal optical disc production and distribution, including China, India, Paraguay, and Vietnam. The United States continues to urge those trading partners who face challenges regarding illegal optical disc production to pass effective legislation to counter this problem, and to enforce existing laws and regulations aggressively.

Finally, the United States encourages trading partners to implement the WIPO Internet Treaties to provide, among other things, protection against the circumvention of technological protection measures and protection for digital rights management information. (*See* Annex 3).

Caribbean copyright challenges

The United States also would like to highlight serious concerns regarding copyright protection and enforcement in the Caribbean region: music licensing and cable and satellite broadcasting. With respect to music licensing, cable operators and television and radio broadcasters in ten countries in the region reportedly refuse to negotiate with performing rights organizations (PROs) for compensation for public performance of music. In some instances, the local governments themselves appear to control these cable operators and broadcasters, such as the Government of Barbados, which owns and operates MCTV, a local cable provider. At the same time, the PROs assert that they have struggled to advance their legal claims in the local courts, which are backlogged and subject to chronic delays. Even where lawsuits have been decided in favor of the PROs, the PROs report that there are difficulties in obtaining final payment. Rights holders in the music industry have repeatedly identified Barbados, Jamaica, and Trinidad and Tobago as the Caribbean region's most problematic markets because of the relative size of their markets. However, a similar pattern of unlicensed cable-casting and broadcasting of copyrighted music reportedly exists in Antigua and Barbuda, Belize, Dominica, Grenada, Guyana, St. Lucia, and St. Vincent and the Grenadines.

With regard to cable and satellite broadcasting of copyrighted television programming, Antigua and Barbuda, Barbados, Belize, Dominica, Grenada, Jamaica, St. Kitts and Nevis, St. Lucia, and St. Vincent and the Grenadines currently maintain a statutory licensing regime that includes a requirement to pay royalties to rights holders. Rights holders assert, however, that they have not received royalty payments from any company in any country in the region, with the notable exception of payments made in 2013 by the Government of the Bahamas. Others in the region – including Anguilla, the Cayman Islands, Dominica, Montserrat, Saint Maarten, and the Turks and Caicos Islands – do not maintain statutory licensing regimes, and reportedly fail to intercede when unauthorized companies intercept and retransmit copyrighted content without remuneration. Again, it is important to note that some of these cable companies are currently or formerly government-owned and operated.

The United States urges these governments to address these issues, and looks forward to engaging on these challenges with the Caribbean Community and Common Market (CARICOM), the Organization of Eastern Caribbean States (OECS), and their member governments.

U.S. concerns with respect to music licensing and unauthorized and uncompensated retransmission of copyright-protected content are not limited to Caribbean markets. We will also engage with other trading partners whose markets present similar challenges.

Government Use of Software

Under Executive Order 13103 issued in September 1998, U.S. Government agencies maintain policies and procedures to ensure that they use only authorized business software. Pursuant to the same directive, USTR has undertaken an initiative to work with other governments, particularly in countries that are modernizing their software systems or where concerns have been raised, to stop unauthorized government use of software. Considerable progress has been made under this initiative, leading to numerous trading partners' mandating that only authorized, legitimate software may be used by their government bodies. Further work on this issue remains with certain trading partners, such as China, Costa Rica, India, Morocco, Pakistan, Paraguay, Saudi Arabia, Thailand, Ukraine, and Vietnam. The United States urges trading partners to adopt and implement effective and transparent procedures to ensure legitimate governmental use of software.

Trademark Issues and Domain Name Disputes

Trademarks help consumers distinguish a company's products and services from competing products and services, and thereby serve a critical source identification role. The goodwill represented in a company's trademarks is often one of the company's most valuable business assets. However, in numerous countries legal and procedural obstacles exist to securing and enforcing trademark rights. Additionally, many countries lack transparency and consistency in administrative registration procedures. In other countries, governments often do not provide the full range of internationally-recognized trademark protections. For example, dozens of countries do not offer a certification mark system for use by foreign or domestic industries. The lack of a certification mark system can make it more difficult to secure protection for products with a quality or characteristic that consumers associate with the product's geographic origin.

Another area of concern for trademark holders is the protection of their trademarks against unauthorized uses under top level domain extensions. U.S. rights holders face significant trademark infringement and loss of valuable Internet traffic because of such uses. A related and growing concern is that certain country code top level domain names (ccTLD) lack transparent and predictable uniform domain name dispute resolution policies (UDRPs). Effective UDRPs should assist in the quick and efficient resolution of these disputes. The United States encourages its trading partners to provide procedures that allow for the protection of trademarks used in domain names, and to ensure that dispute resolution procedures are available to prevent the misuse of trademarks.

Geographical Indications

The United States is working intensively through bilateral and multilateral channels to advance U.S. market access interests and to ensure that the trade initiatives of other countries, including with respect to geographical indications (GIs), do not undercut U.S. industries' market access. GIs typically consist of place names (or words associated with a place) and they identify products or services as having a particular quality, reputation, or other characteristic attributable to their geographic origin.

The U.S. Government is actively involved in promoting and protecting access to foreign markets for U.S. exporters whose products are identified by common names or generic terms, like parmesan and mozzarella for cheese. The United States is pressing its objectives in a variety of contexts, including in the WTO, WIPO and Asia-Pacific Economic Cooperation (APEC) as well as in our bilateral agreements. The United States is also engaging bilaterally to address GI-related concerns, including with Canada, China, Colombia, Costa Rica, El Salvador, the European Union and its Member States, and the Philippines, among others. U.S. goals in this regard include:

- Ensuring that grants of GI protection do not violate prior rights (for example, in cases in which a U.S. company has a trademark that includes a place name);

- Ensuring that grants of GI protection do not deprive interested parties of the ability to use generic or common terms, such as parmesan or mozzarella;

- Ensuring that interested persons have notice of, and opportunity to oppose, or to seek cancellation of, any GI protection that is sought or granted; and

- Opposing efforts to amend the TRIPS Agreement to extend to other products the special protection that is provided to GIs for wines and spirits.

Intellectual Property and Health Policy

Numerous comments in the 2014 Special 301 review highlighted concerns arising at the intersection of IPR policy and health policy.

Intellectual property plays an important role in providing the incentives necessary for the development and marketing of new medicines. An effective, transparent, and predictable IP system is necessary for both manufacturers of innovative medicines and manufacturers of generic medicines.

The 2001 WTO Doha Declaration on the TRIPS Agreement and Public Health recognized the gravity of the public health problems afflicting many developing and least-developed countries, especially those resulting from HIV/AIDS, tuberculosis, malaria, and other epidemics. As affirmed in the Doha Declaration on the TRIPS Agreement and Public Health, the United States respects a trading partner's right to protect public health and, in particular, to promote access to medicines for all. The United States also recognizes the role of IP protection in the development of new medicines, while being mindful of the effect of IP protection on prices. The assessments set forth in this Report are based on various critical factors, including, where relevant, the Doha Declaration on the TRIPS Agreement and Public Health.

The United States is firmly of the view that international obligations such as those in the TRIPS Agreement have sufficient flexibility to allow trading partners to address the serious public health problems that they may face. Consistent with this view, the United States respects its trading partners' rights to grant compulsory licenses in a manner consistent with the provisions of the TRIPS Agreement and the Doha Declaration on the TRIPS Agreement and Public Health, and encourages its trading partners to consider ways to address their public health challenges while maintaining IPR systems that promote innovation.

The United States also strongly supports the WTO General Council Decision on the Implementation of Paragraph 6 of the Doha Declaration on the TRIPS Agreement and Public Health concluded in August 2003. Under this decision, Members are permitted, in accordance with specified procedures, to issue compulsory licenses to export pharmaceutical products to countries that cannot produce drugs for themselves. The WTO General Council adopted a Decision in December 2005 that incorporated this solution into an amendment to the TRIPS Agreement, and the United States became the first WTO Member to formally accept this amendment. The United States hopes that at least two-thirds of the WTO membership accept this amendment by the current deadline, December 31, 2015, at which point the amendment will go into effect for those Members. The August 2003 waiver will remain in place and available until the amendment takes effect.

The United States will work to ensure that the provisions of its bilateral and regional trade agreements, as well as U.S. engagement in international organizations, including the United Nations and related institutions such as WIPO and the WHO, are consistent with U.S. Government policies concerning IPR and health policy and do not impede its trading partners from taking measures necessary to protect public health. Accordingly, USTR will continue its close cooperation with relevant agencies to ensure that public health challenges are addressed and IPR protection and enforcement are supported as one of various mechanisms to promote research and innovation.

Supporting Pharmaceutical and Medical Device Innovation through Improved Market Access

Among other mechanisms to support pharmaceutical and medical device innovation, USTR has sought to reduce market access barriers, including those that discriminate against U.S. companies or are not adequately transparent, in order to facilitate both affordable health care today and the innovation that assures improved health care tomorrow. This year's Special 301 Report highlights concerns regarding market access barriers affecting pharmaceutical and medical device products, particularly in Algeria, Indonesia, and India.

Measures, including those that are discriminatory, nontransparent or otherwise trade-restrictive, have the potential to hinder market access in the pharmaceutical and medical device sector, and potentially result in higher healthcare costs. For example, taxes or tariffs may be levied – often in a non-transparent manner – on imported medicines and the increased expense associated with those levies is then passed directly to healthcare institutions and patients. The United States notes that, according to an October 2012 WTO report titled *More Trade for Better Health? International Trade and Tariffs on Health Products*, India maintains the highest tariffs on medicines, inputs to medicines, and medical devices among the WTO members identified in the report. These tariffs, combined with other internal charges or measures, such as price controls that appear to exempt domestically developed and manufactured medicines, can hinder the Indian government's efforts to promote increased access to healthcare products.

Moreover, unreasonable regulatory approval delays and non-transparent reimbursement policies can impede a company's ability to exercise its IP rights, and thereby discourage the development and marketing of new drugs and other medical products. The criteria, rationale, and operation of such measures are often nontransparent or not fully disclosed to patients or to pharmaceutical and medical device companies seeking to market their products. USTR encourages trading partners to provide appropriate mechanisms for transparency, procedural and due process protections, and opportunities for public engagement in the context of their relevant health care systems.

U.S. industry has expressed concerns regarding the policies of several trading partners, including Finland, Germany, Greece, Hungary, Italy, Korea, New Zealand, Poland, Portugal, Romania, Spain, Turkey, and Taiwan, on issues related to innovation in the pharmaceutical sector and other aspects of health care goods and services. Examples include:

- With respect to New Zealand, U.S. industry has expressed serious concerns about the policies and operation of New Zealand's Pharmaceutical Management Agency (PhARMAC), including, among other things, the lack of transparency, fairness, and predictability of the PhARMAC pricing and reimbursement regime, as well as the negative aspects of the overall climate for innovative medicines in New Zealand; and

- With respect to Turkey, U.S. industry continues to express significant concern regarding the lack of fairness and the slow pace of pharmaceutical manufacturing inspections.

The United States is seeking to establish or continue dialogues with relevant trading partners to address these and other concerns, and encourage a common understanding on questions related to innovation in the pharmaceutical and medical device sectors. The United States also looks forward to continuing its engagement with China, India, and other trading partners to promote fair and transparent policies in this sector.

The United States, like many countries, faces healthcare challenges, including with respect to aging populations and rising health care costs. The United States shares the objective of continued improvement in the health and quality of life of its citizens, and the objective of delivering efficient, responsive, and cost-effective high-quality health care to its population. The United States looks forward to engaging with its trading partners on the concerns noted above.

Implementation of the WTO TRIPS Agreement

The TRIPS Agreement, one of the most significant achievements of the Uruguay Round (1986-1995), requires all WTO Members to provide certain minimum standards of IPR protection and enforcement. The TRIPS Agreement is the first broadly-subscribed multilateral IPR agreement that is subject to mandatory dispute settlement provisions.

Developed country Members were required to implement the TRIPS Agreement fully as of January 1, 1996. Developing country Members were given a transition period for many obligations until January 1, 2000, and in some cases, until January 1, 2005. Nevertheless, certain Members are still in the process of finalizing implementing legislation, and many are still engaged in establishing adequate and effective IPR enforcement mechanisms.

Recognizing the particular challenges faced by least-developed country (LDC) Members, the United States has worked closely with them and other WTO Members to extend the implementation date for these countries. On June 11, 2013, the TRIPS Council reached consensus on a decision to again extend the transition period under Article 66.1 of the TRIPS Agreement for LDC Members. Under this decision, LDC Members are not required to apply the provisions of the TRIPS Agreement, other than Articles 3, 4 and 5, until July 1, 2021, or until such a date on which they cease to be a LDC Member, whichever date is earlier. Additionally, the LDC Members have until 2016 to implement their TRIPS Agreement obligations for patent and data protection for pharmaceutical products, as proposed by the United States at the Doha Ministerial Conference of the WTO.

The United States participates actively in the WTO TRIPS Council's scheduled reviews of WTO Members' implementation of the TRIPS Agreement and also uses the WTO's Trade Policy Review mechanism to pose questions and seek constructive engagement on issues related to TRIPS Agreement implementation.

WTO Dispute Settlement

The United States continues to monitor the resolution of disputes announced in previous Special 301 reviews. The most efficient and preferred manner of resolving concerns is through bilateral dialogue. Where these efforts are unsuccessful, the United States will not hesitate to use the WTO dispute settlement procedures, as appropriate.

In April 2007, the United States initiated dispute settlement procedures relating to deficiencies in China's legal regime for protecting and enforcing copyrights and trademarks on a wide range of products. In March 2009, the WTO Dispute Settlement Body (DSB) adopted a panel report that upheld two of the claims advanced by the United States, finding that (1) China's denial of copyright protection to works that do not meet China's content review standards is impermissible under the TRIPS Agreement; and (2) China's customs rules cannot allow seized counterfeit goods to be publicly auctioned after only removing the infringing mark. With respect to a third claim concerning China's thresholds for criminal prosecution and conviction of counterfeiting and piracy, while the United States prevailed on the interpretation of the important legal standards in Article 61 of the TRIPS Agreement, including the finding that criminal enforcement measures must reflect and respond to the realities of the commercial marketplace, the panel found that it needed additional evidence before it could uphold the overall U.S. claim that China's criminal thresholds are too high. On March 19, 2010, China announced that it had completed all the necessary domestic legislative procedures to implement the DSB recommendations and rulings. The United States continues to monitor China's implementation of the DSB recommendations and rulings in this dispute.

In addition, the United States requested WTO dispute settlement consultations with China concerning certain other Chinese measures affecting market access and distribution for imported publications, movies, and music, and audio-visual home entertainment products (*e.g.*, DVDs, Blu-ray discs, *etc.*) (AVHE products). The U.S. claims challenged China's prohibition on foreign companies' importation of all products at issue; China's prohibitions and discriminatory requirements imposed on foreign distributors of publications, music, and AVHE products within China; and China's imposition of more burdensome requirements on the distribution of imported publications, movies, and music vis-à-vis their domestic counterparts. On January 19, 2010, the DSB adopted panel and Appellate Body reports that found in favor of the United States on the vast majority of its claims. China committed to bring all relevant measures into compliance with the DSB recommendations by March 19, 2011, and subsequently revised or revoked several measures relating to publications, AVHE products, and music. China did not issue any measures relating to theatrical films, but instead proposed bilateral discussions. The United States and China reached agreement in February 2012 on the terms of a Memorandum of Understanding that provides significantly increased market access for imported films and significantly improved compensation for foreign film producers. The United States continues to review and monitor the steps that China has taken toward compliance in this matter.

Following the 1999 Special 301 review, the United States initiated dispute settlement consultations concerning the EU regulation on food-related GIs, which appeared to discriminate against foreign products and persons, notably by requiring that EU trading partners adopt an "EU-style" system of GI protection, and appeared to provide insufficient protections to trademark owners. On April 20, 2005, the DSB adopted a panel report finding in favor of the United States that the EU GI regulation is inconsistent with the EU's obligations under the TRIPS Agreement and the General Agreement on Tariffs and Trade 1994. On March 31, 2006, the EU published a revised GI Regulation that is intended to comply with the DSB recommendations and rulings. There remain some concerns, however, with respect to this revised GI Regulation, which the United States has asked the EU to address, and the United States intends to continue monitoring this situation. The United States is also working intensively through bilateral and multilateral fora to advance U.S. market access interests, and to ensure that the trade initiatives of other countries, including with respect to GIs, do not undercut our market access.

Interagency Trade Enforcement Center

In his State of the Union address on January 24, 2012, President Obama announced the creation of the Interagency Trade Enforcement Center (ITEC) to take a whole-of-government approach to monitoring and enforcing Americans' trade rights around the world. Thereafter, on February 28, 2012, the President issued an Executive Order that established ITEC. As the federal government's primary coordinator of international and domestic trade enforcement, ITEC helps to ensure that America's trading partners abide by their obligations, including by maintaining open markets on a non-discriminatory basis, and by following rules-based procedures in a transparent way. ITEC leverages and mobilizes the federal government's resources and expertise to address unfair foreign trade practices and barriers. In particular, ITEC uses expertise from across the federal government to assist in asserting U.S. trade rights implicated by various international trade agreements and serves as the primary forum within the federal government for agencies to coordinate enforcement of obligations under international trade agreements, including the identification of unfair trade practices and barriers that involve IPR.

SECTION II. COUNTRY REPORTS

Determination in Section 301 Investigation of Ukraine

Ukraine was designated a Priority Foreign Country in the 2013 Special Report due to the particular IPR acts, policies, and practices identified in the 2013 Special 301 Report. (*See* 2013 Special 301 Report; Identification of Ukraine as a Priority Foreign Country and Initiation of Section 301 Investigation, 78 FR 33886 (June 5, 2013)). Those acts, policies, and practices involved: (1) the administration of Ukraine's system for collecting societies, which are responsible for collecting and distributing copyright royalties to U.S. and other rights holders; (2) use of infringing software by Ukrainian government agencies; and (3) online infringement of copyright and related rights. On May 30, 2013, the United States Trade Representative initiated a Section 301 investigation of the acts, policies, and practices identified in the Special 301 Report.

Based on the information obtained during the investigation, on February 28, 2014, the U.S. Trade Representative determined that these acts, policies, and practices are unreasonable and burden or restrict United States commerce, but, due to the current political situation in Ukraine, no action would be taken at that time. (*See* Notice of Determination in Section 301 Investigation of Ukraine, 79 FR 14326 (March 13, 2014)).

USTR remains committed to addressing the problems that served as the basis for the designation of Ukraine as a PFC, and appreciates Ukraine's recent outreach and ongoing engagement in exploring how to ameliorate these problems and improve its overall IP regime. The United States looks forward to working with Ukraine on these three issues.

PRIORITY WATCH LIST

China

China remains on the Priority Watch List and subject to Section 306 monitoring.

China's leadership has acknowledged the critical role that intellectual property plays in spurring innovation and the need to improve China's protection and enforcement of IP rights, including at the Third Plenum of the 18th Central Committee of the Chinese Communist Party. Consistent with China's policy objectives, its judicial, legislative, administrative, and enforcement authorities are in the midst of wide-ranging legal reform efforts relating to the protection and enforcement of IPR in China. Certain rights holders report positive experiences, including in some cases a greater ability to obtain redress against infringers in civil court actions. The United States also notes increased cooperation between U.S. and Chinese law enforcement agencies in an effort to stem cross-border flows of infringing products. The United States looks forward to strengthened cooperation, building on the increasing and positive cooperation between U.S. customs and investigative agencies and their Chinese counterparts, including the General Administration of Customs and Ministry of Public Security.

At the same time, a wide range of U.S. stakeholders in China continues to report serious obstacles to effective protection of IPR in all forms, including patents, copyrights, trademarks, trade secrets as well as protection against unfair commercial use or unauthorized disclosure of test and other data generated to obtain marketing approval for pharmaceutical products. As a result, sales of IPR-intensive goods and services in China remain disproportionately low when compared to sales in similar, or even less developed, markets that provide a stronger environment for IPR protection and market access. Despite laudable policy objectives and a welcome ongoing reform effort, foreign rights holders in China continue to face a complex and challenging IPR environment. Given the size of China's consumer marketplace and its global importance as a producer of a broad range of products, China's protection and enforcement of IPR will continue to be a focus of U.S. trade policy.

In particular, the theft of trade secrets remains a significant concern. Such thefts are occurring not only inside but also outside China for the competitive advantage of Chinese state-owned and private companies. Conditions are likely to deteriorate as long as those committing such thefts, and those benefitting, continue to operate with relative impunity, often taking advantage of the theft in order to enter into unfair competition or disadvantageous business relationships with their victims. The United States strongly urges the Chinese government to take serious steps to put an end to these activities and to deter further activity by rigorously investigating and prosecuting trade secret thefts conducted by both cyber and conventional means.

Of longstanding concern are Chinese central, provincial, and local government measures and actions that appear to require or pressure rights holders to transfer IPR from foreign to domestic entities. Sometimes guided by government measures or policy statements intended to promote indigenous innovation and the development of strategic industries, government authorities may deny or delay market access or otherwise condition government procurement, permissions, subsidies, tax treatment, and other actions on IPR being owned or developed in China, or licensed to a Chinese entity. The U.S. Government is also concerned by the increased number of stakeholders reporting that Chinese government entities are using regulatory pressure to compel the licensing of important technologies or to dissuade stakeholders from pursuing available legal avenues to enforce their IPR. China has made certain commitments to the United States on some of these matters; the United States will continue pressing China to follow through on those commitments.

Legal Reform

The United States welcomes China's ongoing legal reform efforts despite serious reservations regarding certain measures. Since 2012, China has undertaken revisions to and invited comment on draft revisions to its existing laws on patents, copyrights, trademarks, drug administration, and scientific and technological achievements. Effective January 1, 2013, China's amended Civil Procedure Law includes provisions that may help U.S. rights holders to secure preliminary measures and otherwise enforce their rights in civil court actions. Currently before China's State Council Legislative Affairs Office (SCLAO) are draft amendments to the Copyright Law and Patent Law. In mid-2014, a revised Trademark Law and implementing regulations will go into effect. Amendment of the Anti-Unfair Competition Law (AUCL), unrevised since first entering into force in 1993, is proceeding at a slower pace. While applauding China's consideration of U.S. government and private sector perspectives and experiences as it amends its laws, the United States notes the need to move forward expeditiously with remaining revisions to its IP-related laws, and underscores the urgent need to update and amend the AUCL and related trade secret laws, regulations, and judicial interpretations, including provisions regarding the protection and enforcement of trade secrets.

China also invited comment on draft rules and guidelines on proposed regulations for the remuneration of "service inventions" (i.e., inventions created by an employee as part of his or her employment), rules for anti-monopoly enforcement in the field of intellectual property rights, and patent examination guidelines for utility model and design patents. Several proposed measures raise serious concerns, while others represent a marked improvement over prior drafts. The United States applauds China's openness to receiving comments and looks forward to continuing engagement as future drafts are developed and evaluated, and as the drafts move through the SCLAO and the National People's Congress.

Additional legal reforms require action, including amending the Criminal Law and other relevant measures to address continuing deficiencies in China's criminal IPR enforcement.

National Leading Group

Following the completion of China's 2010-11 Special IPR Campaign, the State Council established a permanent office of the national leading group on combating IPR infringement (Leading Group) to better coordinate and improve China's efforts to combat IPR infringement and the manufacture and sale of counterfeit and sub-standard goods. In 2013, the Leading Group continued to coordinate enforcement actions and undertake special campaigns, including concerning online markets and cross-border infringement cases. The United States encourages China to continue to work with foreign governments and rights holders to share information and demonstrate the constructive role the Leading Group can play to improve the protection and enforcement of IPR.

Trade Secrets

As noted above, trade secret theft is a serious and growing problem in China. Thefts may arise in a variety of circumstances, including those involving departing employees, failed joint ventures, and cyber intrusion and hacking. In addition, thefts arising from the misuse of information submitted to government entities for purposes of complying with regulatory obligations are particularly troubling. The misappropriation of trade secrets and their use by a competing enterprise can have a devastating impact on a company's business, making recourse to adequate and effective legal remedies particularly important.

Under Chinese law, however, available remedies are difficult to obtain, given that civil, administrative, and criminal enforcement against trade secrets theft remains severely constrained. Enforcement obstacles include various deficiencies in China's AUCL; constraints on gathering evidence for use in litigation; difficulties in meeting the criteria for establishing that information constitutes a trade secret; and criminal penalties that do not provide adequate deterrents. Unlike other Chinese IP laws, the AUCL does not expressly authorize judges to issue certain provisional orders that are often critical to the successful pursuit of a civil enforcement action. While China's new Civil Procedure Law may address, or partially address, that problem, there has been insufficient time to ascertain whether this new law is facilitating access to civil remedies in practice. Additionally, the AUCL appears to apply primarily to "commercial undertakings" and not to impose liability on individual actors; the AUCL also requires that a trade secret have "practical applicability," which may limit the scope of protection for early stage research.

There are other important weaknesses in China's civil enforcement system that relate to mechanisms for gathering evidence; procedures for obtaining preliminary injunctions; and the relative weight afforded certain kinds of evidence, as reflected in the overreliance on original documentary evidence over oral testimony. Without changes to address these weaknesses, some of which are not specific to intellectual property but relate to China's civil process generally, effective enforcement against misappropriation of trade secrets in China will remain challenging.

The United States is encouraged by China's December 2013 Joint Commission on Commerce and Trade (JCCT) commitment to undertake an Action Program that will include concrete actions to address enforcement, enhance public awareness, and require strict legal compliance with respect to trade secrets. The United States will continue to engage with China as it develops this Action Program, and as it advances legal and regulatory reforms to better protect trade secrets.

Copyright and Piracy

Software legalization

The United States will continue to urge that all levels of the Chinese government, as well as state-owned enterprises (SOEs), use only legitimate, licensed copies of software. In May 2011, China's government reported that software legalization in central government offices was complete. At the provincial level, China's government reported that a similar effort was completed as of June 30, 2012. In January, 2014, the Chinese government reported that all local government agencies at the city and county level had completed software legalization by the end of 2013. However, even with the significant work to legalize this number and range of government agencies, U.S. software companies have seen only a modest increase in sales to government agencies, and specific information about the procedures and tools used to ascertain budget or audit information remains unavailable.

Software legalization efforts more recently have extended to China's SOE sector. Losses by software companies due to piracy at SOEs and other enterprises remain very high. To the degree that Chinese firms do not pay for the software that runs many of their operations, they reap a cost advantage relative to competitors who pay for legally acquired software. The United States remains committed to working with China to continue to address these challenges.

Online piracy

Despite bilateral commitments to increase IPR enforcement, online piracy in China persists on a large scale. As of 2013, China had the largest Internet user base in the world, estimated at over 600 million users, including nearly 500 million mobile web users. Despite national campaigns and the leadership of the Leading Group, widespread piracy affects industries involved in the distribution of legitimate music, motion pictures, books and journals, video games, and software. For example, industry reports that in 2013 the revenues from digital music sales in China were $65.4 million, compared to $108.3 million in South Korea, and $32.0 million in Thailand – a country with less than five percent of China's population and a roughly equivalent per capita GDP. Similarly, over 90 percent of the revenue generated by U.S. films in China comes in the form of box office revenues, compared to 25-30 percent in the United States. This difference is partly due to widespread piracy of motion pictures over the Internet and on optical discs. Online piracy extends to scientific, technical, and medical publications as well.

Parties in China are also facilitating online infringement, in China and third countries, through media box piracy. Manufactured in China and exported abroad, media boxes can be preloaded with infringing content and plugged directly into televisions. They enable the user to stream and download infringing online audio and visual content. The vast majority of the infringing websites to which media box users connect are reportedly located in China. The United States urges China to continue efforts to improve IPR protection and enforcement in this area.

Counterfeit Goods

Despite increased enforcement efforts, problems with counterfeiting in China remain widespread. A partial list of commonly counterfeited goods includes food and beverages; apparel, footwear, and accessories; consumer electronics, computers and networking equipment; entertainment and business software; batteries; chemicals; appliances; pharmaceuticals; and auto parts. Impacts are not limited to lost sales volumes and damage to the reputation of the trademark owner. For example, higher defect and failure rates among counterfeit semiconductors may cause malfunctions in the equipment in which they are incorporated, which may include medical devices, vehicle safety and braking systems, and other critical applications. As one measure of the scale of the problem, products from China (including Hong Kong) accounted for 93 percent of the value of the IPR infringing products seized by U.S. Customs and Border Protection in fiscal year 2013.

Although rights holders report increased enforcement activities, mostly but not exclusively on behalf of local brands, enforcement efforts have yet to slow the sale of counterfeit products online. This is particularly concerning in light of the rapid growth of e-commerce both within China and between China and overseas markets. Rights holders report that local Administrations for Industry and Commerce (AICs) typically confine their efforts to physical markets. While both the State Administration for Industry and Commerce and local AICs have called on online trading websites to improve procedures to address online sales of counterfeit merchandise, these measures have not significantly deterred repeat and large-scale offenders who, after postings are removed, quickly place new postings offering the same infringing goods. It is reported that the Supreme People's Court may issue a judicial interpretation to address these concerns.

IPR and Technology Transfer Requirements

The United States is concerned about Chinese measures, policies and practices at the national, provincial, and local levels that allegedly are intended to hasten China's development into an innovative economy, but that may disadvantage foreign rights holders. Industry reports that many of China's innovation-related policies and other industrial policies, such as strategic emerging industry policies, may have a negative impact on U.S. exports or U.S. investors and their investments or IP rights. Such Chinese measures frequently call for technology transfer and, in certain cases, appear to include criteria that could require IP rights to be developed in China, or to be owned by or licensed to a Chinese party. Such government-imposed conditions or incentives may distort licensing and other private business arrangements, resulting in commercial outcomes that are not optimal for the firms involved or for promoting innovation. Such government intervention in the commercial decisions that enterprises make regarding the ownership, development, registration, or licensing of IP is not consistent with international practice, and may raise concerns relative to China's implementation of its WTO commitments.

Sustained U.S.-China engagement through the JCCT, the U.S.-China Strategic and Economic Dialogue (S&ED), and high-level government engagement has resulted in important Chinese commitments, including "that technology transfer and technological cooperation shall be decided by businesses independently and will not be used by the Chinese government as a pre-condition for market access," and that China will "treat and protect intellectual property rights (IPR) owned or developed in other countries the same as domestically owned or developed IPR." In addition, at the 2012 JCCT, China "reaffirmed that technology transfer and technology cooperation are the autonomous decisions of enterprises" and pledged further that "[i]f departmental or local documents contain language inconsistent with the above commitment, China will correct them in a timely manner." At the 2013 JCCT, China committed not to implement rules or finalize a draft catalogue containing indigenous innovation criteria for the procurement of vehicles for official use that are inconsistent with China's 2012 JCCT commitment. The United States looks forward to China's full implementation of its commitments, and the revision of other measures, including elements of the High and New Technology Enterprise tax incentive, including requirements that beneficiaries license core IP exclusively to a party in China and make 60 percent of their global research and development expenditures in China.

Patent-Related and Other Policies

IPR and technological standards

The growing importance of IPR and technological standards in China heightens U.S. concerns with a range of Chinese government policies and practices. Whereas open, voluntary, and consensus-based standards best promote economic development, efficiency and innovation, standards development bodies in China often employ opaque and exclusionary practices to the detriment of U.S. and other foreign parties. China's standards setting bodies reportedly often deny membership or participation rights to foreign parties, effectively shutting them out of the process. In some cases, such bodies may condition a firm's ability to participate on it acting through a joint venture in which it can only have a minority ownership stake, the licensing of a firm's IP on concessional terms, or a firm's transfer of technology. Based on a limited number of investigations conducted to date, there is also growing concern that Chinese competition authorities may target for investigation foreign firms that hold IPR that may be essential to the implementation of certain technological standards. Industry reports of intimidating and non-transparent investigative conduct contribute to these concerns. In the related realm of national standards, the Standardization Administration of China (SAC) and the State Intellectual Property Organization (SIPO) published Regulatory Measures on National Standards Involving Patents (Interim) that went into effect on January 1, 2014. The final version of the provisional measures addressed a number of U.S. government and industry concerns with earlier drafts. However, uncertainty remains as to how the measures apply to patent holders who are not participants in the particular standards development process to which the measures apply. In particular, with respect to patents relevant to a particular standard under development, such measures include a provision that encourages non-participant holders of such patents to disclose the patents and provisions regarding requests for licensing declarations from holders of such patents. The United States is concerned by any suggestion that standards-related disclosure and licensing obligations extend to patent holders electing not to participate in standards development.

IPR protection for pharmaceutical products

The United States has engaged intensively with China to address troubling obstacles to obtaining and maintaining patents on pharmaceutical innovations. Although SIPO guidelines governing the review of patent applications were once generally consistent with those of the United States and leading patent offices in other countries, China's revised interpretation severely restricted a patent applicant's ability to provide supplemental information in support of an application. As a result, China has denied pharmaceutical patent applications and invalidated existing patents, even with respect to applications and patents consistently awarded by U.S. and other patent offices. This problem was the subject of great attention during Vice President Biden's visit to Beijing in November 2013 and the annual meeting of the JCCT the following month. These engagements resulted in China's revision of the policy on information supplementation, and a commitment to work with the United States to follow up on implementation, including the examination of individual cases.

In addition, the United States continues to have concerns about the extent to which China provides effective protection against unfair commercial use, as well as unauthorized disclosure of undisclosed test or other data generated to obtain marketing approval for pharmaceutical products. Under Chinese law and international commitments, China is required to ensure that no subsequent applicant may rely on the undisclosed test or other data submitted in support of an application for marketing approval of new pharmaceutical products for a period of at least six years from the date of marketing approval in China. However, there are reports that generic manufacturers have been granted marketing approvals by the China Food and Drug Administration (CFDA) prior to the expiration of this period, and in some cases, even before the originator's product has been approved. The United States was encouraged by China's 2012 JCCT commitment to define "new chemical entity," a term that is central to the marketing approval process, in a manner consistent with international practice. Given that more than a year has passed since that time, the United States is urging China to implement its commitment without delay.

On November 12, 2013, CFDA invited comment on draft amendments to the Drug Registration Rules (DRR). The United States and industry expressed concern that the proposed deletion of Article 19 from the DRR would weaken regulatory pharmaceutical patent enforcement. CFDA subsequently issued a revised draft that retained Article 19, albeit in modified form. The United States will continue to engage with China on this and other issues.

Utility model and design patents

For years, the U.S. Government and U.S. rights holders have expressed concerns about the quality of China's utility model and design patents, which SIPO grants without substantive examination and which China encourages through subsidies and other incentives. The poor quality of many of these patents has led to abusive litigation, and burdens on legitimate businesses seeking to make patentability or freedom to operate determinations. After receiving comments on a prior draft, amendments to SIPO's patent examination guidelines for utility model and design patents came into force on October 15, 2013. Although the new guidelines do not require substantive examination, they permit examiners to gather additional information in certain cases at their discretion. The impact of the recent change is still difficult to assess, but the amendments appears to be a welcome initial step.

On May 1, 2014, new SIPO examination guidelines take effect allowing the grant of design patents on graphical user interfaces (GUIs). This welcome step comes after sustained U.S. engagement, although the impact of certain provisions in the guidelines pose the potential to undermine at least some of the apparent gains.

The United States looks forward to continuing to work with China to resolve these and other issues.

India

India remains on the Priority Watch List in 2014. In making this determination, the United States recognizes not only the concerns listed below, but also the critical role that meaningful, constructive, and effective engagement between India and the United States should play in resolving these concerns. Serious difficulties in attaining constructive engagement on issues of concern to U.S. and other stakeholders have contributed to India's challenging environment for IPR protection and enforcement. In the coming months, the United States will redouble its efforts to seek opportunities for meaningful, sustained, and effective engagement on IP-related matters with the new government, including at senior levels and through technical exchanges, that will both improve IP protection and enforcement in India, and support India's efforts to achieve a "Decade of Innovation" and advance its legitimate public policy goals. These opportunities include strengthening IP-related discussions between U.S. and Indian government officials; facilitating regular exchanges among IP-intensive industries and both governments; initiating cooperative efforts to combat piracy; and working with the Government of India to encourage the private sector to establish an IP-related task force under the U.S.-India CEO Forum. To further encourage progress on IPR issues of concern, USTR will publish a *Federal Register* notice and initiate an Out-of-Cycle Review (OCR) of India in the fall of 2014, commencing an assessment of the progress in that engagement.

In 2013, India made some limited progress in improving its weak IPR legal framework and enforcement system. India acceded to and implemented the Madrid Protocol; continued progress toward digitization of cable networks to help efforts to combat signal theft by cable operators; and enacted rules to implement amendments to its Copyright Act. 2013 also saw more active copyright enforcement by the Delhi High Court through the issuance of Ashok Kumar and Anton Piller orders, which provide injunctive relief to rights holders.

In many areas, however, IP protection and enforcement challenges are growing, and there are serious questions regarding the future of the innovation climate in India across multiple sectors and disciplines. In fact, many of the submissions made by a wide array of stakeholders in this year's Special 301 reporting process underscored increasing challenges rights holders face in India, and a number of those submissions sought the strongest censure of India's IP environment available under Special 301. The United States urges India to take specific actions to address the concerns raised, including by means of constructive bilateral engagement. The United States also urges India to reconsider how to meet its legitimate domestic policy objectives while fostering a climate for innovation. The United States continues to encourage India to strengthen civil IPR enforcement by increasing judicial efficiency and reducing court backlogs through electronic case management, fast-track procedures, specialized judges, and similar reform measures. In addition, the United States supports India's efforts to initiate criminal investigations and launch raids at counterfeit goods markets; combat the manufacture, sale and distribution of counterfeit medicines; initiate investigations and judicial actions against Internet piracy; and seek deterrent sentences against persons or entities engaging in copyright piracy and trademark counterfeiting.

Copyright and Piracy

India boasts a vibrant domestic creative industry, but it faces a range of challenges, including growing piracy, particularly over the Internet, that should be addressed through appropriate legal and enforcement reforms. The United States continues to seek additional changes to the amended Copyright Act and related rules that went into effect in 2013. These changes would help resolve questions regarding the scope of exclusive rights under Indian law and the ability of rights holders to exercise those rights. They would also help ensure that content-based industries can effectively combat physical and online piracy and develop new models for the delivery of content, particularly in the digital environment. The United States encourages India, as part of its copyright and enforcement reforms, to enact anti-camcording legislation; to model its statutory license provisions relating to copyrighted works upon Berne Convention standards; to ensure that collecting societies are licensed promptly and able to operate effectively; and to provide additional protections against signal theft, circumvention of technological protection measures, and online copyright piracy.

The United States is particularly concerned over online piracy in India given the size and growth of India's market. According to a report by McKinsey & Company, as of December 2012, India's Internet user base was the third largest in the world, with 120 million users, and by 2015, India will have the world's second largest user base, estimated at 330-370 million Internet users. This trend makes it all the more imperative that India incorporate into its legal system more effective measures to counter online piracy, including appropriate notice-and-takedown procedures and other efficient mechanisms for rights holders to seek removal of infringing content from websites, consistent with international best practices.

The high incidence of camcording in India underscores the importance of developing an effective legal framework to address this problem. India has one of the highest rates of video piracy in the world, according to the Motion Pictures Distributors Association of India (MPDA). Moreover, according to the Motion Picture Association (MPA), camcording incidents involving motion pictures produced by MPA member studios alone have risen rapidly over the past few years, with 155 forensic matches traced to India from 2009 to 2011. In 2013 alone, there were reportedly 43 such forensic matches, accounting for approximately half of all such incidents in the Asia-Pacific in that year. These incidents do not take into account camcording of films produced by non-MPA members, including many films produced in India and elsewhere in the world. The United States welcomes statements made by the Ministry of Information and Broadcasting that it plans to include specific anti-camcording provisions in the draft Cinematographic Bill, and the support of the government of Andhra Pradesh that helped launch in 2013 the India Movie Cop app developed by that state's film industry.

The United States notes limited improvements with respect to copyright enforcement, including reports that enforcement officials cooperate with music industry rights holders in conducting complaint-based raids, and increased use of judicial orders that have strengthened enforcement against pirated movies and music online. The United States encourages India to take additional steps to improve coordination with enforcement officials of state governments within India.

To strengthen engagement on these and other copyright issues, and to build upon the strengths of the vibrant Indian and U.S. copyright-intensive industries, including in movies, music, and software, the United States would welcome closer bilateral cooperation with India in addressing the challenges of copyright piracy of U.S. and Indian content globally, including, for example, cooperation and exchanges at the technical level between copyright protection and enforcement experts in each government.

Patents & Regulatory Data Protection

The United States continues to encourage India to promote a stable and predictable patent system that nurtures and incentivizes innovation. As leading economies with a strong tradition of innovation, India and the United States can and should ensure supportive environments for innovators to achieve success and make significant contributions to economic growth in both countries.

The United States commends India on actions taken in recent years to improve the operations of its Patent Office, including digitizing records, upgrading online search and e-filing capabilities, and hiring additional patent examiners. The United States urges India to continue its recent efforts to address its patent application backlog. The United States welcomes recent statements from India's Controller-General of Patents regarding plans to hire 500 patent examiners in the next five years, as well as a Delhi High Court decision ordering a committee of senior officials to develop a plan of action to address the backlog and ensure that future applications are processed within the statutory deadline. The United States encourages greater technical collaboration between patent authorities in both countries that would facilitate the more timely examination of patent applications.

Recent actions by the Government of India with respect to patents, however, have raised serious concerns about the innovation climate in India and risk hindering India's progress towards an innovation-focused economy. In the pharmaceutical sector and increasingly in other sectors, such as the agro-chemicals and green technology sectors, some innovators face serious challenges in securing and enforcing patents in India. In recognition of the fact that an environment conducive to the protection and enforcement of IP can help to address pressing domestic policy challenges, the United States encourages India to adopt policies that support both cutting-edge innovation to address important health challenges and a robust generic market.

For example, a patent system should encourage the development of inventions that meet the well-established international criteria of being new, involving an inventive step, and being capable of industrial application, including as provided for in the TRIPS Agreement. Under India's Patents Act, a patent is available for an "invention," defined in Section 2(j) of the Act as a product or process that is novel, has an inventive step, and is capable of industrial application. Section 3(d) of India's Patent Act states in relevant part that "the mere discovery of a new form of a known substance which does not result in the enhancement of the known efficacy of that substance" is not considered to be an "invention" under Indian law.[1] As the Indian Supreme

---

[1] Section 3(d) contains a further *Explanation* stating that "[f]or the purposes of this clause [3(d)], salts, esthers, ethers, polymorphs, metabolites, pure form, particle size, isomers, mixtures of isomers, complexes, combinations and other derivatives of known substance shall be considered to be the same substance, unless they differ significantly in properties with regard to efficacy."

Court recently explained, in the case of patent applications for pharmaceuticals and other chemicals:

> The amended portion of section 3(d) clearly sets up a *second tier* of qualifying standards for chemical substances/pharmaceutical products in order to leave the door open for true and genuine inventions …. [O]n reading [section 2] with section 3(d) it would appear that the Act sets *different standards* for qualifying as 'inventions' things belonging to different classes, and for medicines and drugs and other chemical substances, the Act *sets the invention threshold higher*, by virtue of [section 3(d)]. … [I]n case of chemicals and especially pharmaceuticals if the product for which patent protection is claimed is a new form of a known substance with known efficacy, then the subject product must pass, *in addition to clauses (j) and (ja) of section 2(1),* the test of enhanced efficacy as provided in section 3(d) read with its explanation.[2]

The United States is concerned that section 3(d), as interpreted, may have the effect of limiting the patentability of potentially beneficial innovations. Such innovations would include drugs with fewer side effects, decreased toxicity, improved delivery systems, or temperature or storage stability. In practice, this standard has already been applied to deny patent protections to potentially beneficial innovations, some of which enjoy patent protection in multiple other jurisdictions.

Even after a product receives a patent, Indian law continues to pose challenges to the enjoyment of that IPR protection.

First, the United States supports patent systems that incorporate efficient patent procedures and foster high-quality patents, and, in that connection, urges India to improve and streamline its patent opposition procedures. Specifically, under India's patent regime, the same interested person may, at minimal cost, challenge a patent through *both* pre-grant and post-grant opposition proceedings on any of eleven enumerated grounds, including by citing the same grounds in both pre- and post-grant challenges. As a result, applications can be tied up in costly challenge proceedings for years, all the while running the potential term of the patent which begins from the application filing date, thus impeding an applicant's ability to make investments and conduct business.

Second, while bearing in mind the Doha Declaration on TRIPS and Public Health, discussed in the Intellectual Property and Health Policy section of this Report, the United States also continues to monitor developments concerning compulsory licensing of patents in India. The United States urges India to provide greater transparency about its ongoing inter-ministerial process that is considering over a dozen patented medicines as candidates for government-initiated compulsory licenses, and urges India to allow opportunities for input by rights holders, as appropriate, with respect to decisions concerning compulsory licenses.

In addition, the United States continues to be concerned with the rationale underlying a decision by India's Controller-General of Patents to grant a compulsory license under Section 84 of India's Patents Act (which allows private parties to initiate proceedings seeking a compulsory

---

[2] *Novartis AG v. Union of India & Others,* Civ. App. Nos. 2706-2716 (Supreme Court, April 1, 2013), paragraphs 103, 104, and 192 (emphasis added).

license of a patented article), as upheld by a recent judgment of the IPAB. The grant of the compulsory license was based, in part, on the innovator's failure to "work" the patent in India because it imported its products, rather than manufacturing them in India. The United States recognizes that, on appeal, the IPAB modified the Controller-General's reasoning to clarify that "in some cases" the "working" requirement could be met solely by importation. The IPAB, however, rejected the innovator's explanation that economic factors prevented manufacturing in India, stating, "the patentee must show why it could not be locally manufactured. A mere statement to that effect is not sufficient[,] there must be evidence."[3] The IPAB did not clarify the circumstances under which the "working" requirement would be met without manufacturing in India. The decision could inappropriately pressure innovators outside of India – including those in sectors well beyond pharmaceuticals, such as green technology and information and communications technology – to manufacture in India in order to avoid being compelled to license an invention to third parties. The IPAB's decision is currently on appeal to the Bombay High Court.

Although the government has issued only one compulsory license under Section 84, India has made clear that it views compulsory licensing as an important tool of industrial policy for green technologies, with the potential to be applied more regularly across economic sectors. Specifically, India has promoted compulsory licensing in its National Manufacturing Policy as a mechanism available for government entities to effectuate technology transfer in the clean energy sector. India similarly has sought to multilateralize this approach in ongoing negotiations under the UNFCCC. In those negotiations India continues to identify patents as obstacles to the dissemination of climate change technologies, pressing for outcomes that would potentially undermine incentives for innovation, such as existing global standards for patent protection that is a critical part of the response to climate change and other environmental challenges.

The United States also notes with concern the continuing challenges involved with enforcement of patent rights in India, including challenges that patent holders face in securing injunctions against firms that manufacture patented inventions without authorization from the patent holder. Additionally, when approving such manufacture without authorization, Indian state governmental authorities reportedly do not have a mechanism to confirm whether the item to be manufactured is under patent. Recent cases such as *Merck v. Glenmark* and *Cipla v. Roche* illustrate this problem and underscore the need for greater regulatory coordination between officials in state and central governments.

Finally, the United States also urges India to provide an effective system for protecting against unfair commercial use, as well as unauthorized disclosure, of undisclosed test or other data generated to obtain marketing approval for pharmaceutical and agricultural chemical products, and to ensure that such a system applies to all pharmaceutical products and not just traditional Indian medicines. It is noteworthy, however, that the Pesticides Management Bill, currently before Parliament, includes provisions for data protection of *agricultural* chemicals for five years, although that time period begins with the product's first marketing approval anywhere in the world. Meanwhile, data protection for *pharmaceuticals* remains under consideration by the Ministry of Health and Family Welfare. Without these types of protections in place against the unfair commercial use of clinical test data, companies in India reportedly are able to copy certain

---

3 Decision of the Intellectual Property Appellate Board, Chennai, March 4, 2013, OA/35/2012/PT/MUM, Paragraph 52

pharmaceutical products and seek immediate government approval for marketing based on the original developer's data.

Trademarks and Counterfeiting

The United States continues to observe significant delays associated with cancellation and opposition proceedings at the administrative level of the Trademark Registry, which are exacerbated by delays in India's judicial processes. While opposition and cancellation proceedings are complex matters that require careful consideration, the reported backlog of more than 160,000 cases represents a significant challenge for companies trying to invest and build brands in India. These delays undermine enforcement mechanisms and their ability to discourage infringing conduct. The United States urges India to take steps to expedite proceedings before the Trademark Registry.

Additionally, the production, sale, distribution, import, and export of counterfeit goods in India remains very troubling. In a study published in September 2013 by the International Chamber of Commerce and the Federation of Indian Chambers of Commerce and Industry analyzing seven key industry sectors vulnerable to counterfeiting and smuggling (automotive parts, alcohol, computer hardware, personal goods, packaged foods, mobile phones, and tobacco products), researchers concluded that unauthorized counterfeiting and smuggling caused average sales losses to right holders of 21.7 percent or approximately $11.9 billion in 2012. Collectively, the Indian government's economic loss tied to these illicit activities totaled approximately $4.26 billion, according to the study. This problem is particularly troubling with respect to the production and distribution of counterfeit pharmaceuticals. While India is one of the world's largest producers of legitimate, high-quality generic pharmaceuticals, and the United States is India's largest single export market for generic pharmaceuticals, India is also the top supplier of counterfeit pharmaceuticals to the United States, according to U.S. Customs and Border Protection data and analysis.

Trade Secrets

The United States is increasingly concerned about trade secret protection in India, particularly the reported difficulty in obtaining remedies and damages. India appears to rely primarily upon the law of contract to provide trade secret protection. Although India's contract-based approach may address the theft of trade secrets where a contract has been breached, India's approach may be less effective in covering situations in which there is no contractual relationship, such as in cases of theft by a business competitor. Although Indian law does provide for some remedies, including injunctive relief, in practice, damages can be very difficult to obtain. Finally, because India's court system reportedly lacks sufficient procedural safeguards to protect trade secrets or other confidential information divulged through discovery in civil or criminal litigation, there is a risk that such information may be disclosed publicly in the course of judicial proceedings.

Localization Trends

The United States commends India's recognition of the importance of innovation in connection with its efforts to promote manufacturing, but urges India to resist imposing discriminatory or other trade-restrictive measures in pursuit of that objective at the expense of adequate and effective protection of IPR. The United States welcomes India's decision to revise the Preferential Market Access (PMA) policy, which previously contained elements that appeared to treat India-owned IP more favorably than foreign-owned IP. The United States remains concerned, however, about actions and policies in India that appear to favor local manufacturing or Indian IP owners in a manner that distorts the competitive landscape needed to ensure the development of globally successful and innovative industries. For example, last year's Drug Price Control Order (DPCO) imposes pricing restrictions on the sale of 348 medicines, but provides exemptions from those restrictions—that is, allows them to be priced at higher levels— for certain medicines that are manufactured in India and "developed using indigenous Research and Development." In addition, as noted above, the IPAB's interpretation of Section 84 of India's Patents Act suggests that a patent could be subject to a compulsory license if it is not manufactured in India.

The United States looks forward to continuing to work with India to address these and other issues.

Russia

Russia remains on the Priority Watch List in 2014 as a result of continued, significant challenges to IPR protection and enforcement. Russia passed amendments to its Civil Code that substantially weakened protections for industrial designs and introduced confusion into the available scope of copyright exceptions and limitations.

The United States is troubled that IPR enforcement continued to decrease overall in 2013, following a dramatic decline in 2012, and remained plagued by a lack of transparency and effectiveness. Stakeholders express concern about the manufacture, transshipment and retail availability of counterfeit goods, including counterfeits of agricultural chemicals, electronics, information technology, auto parts, consumer goods, machinery, and other products. Enforcement actions combatting end user piracy have sharply declined, including a decrease in raids, initiations of criminal cases, and issuances of court verdicts.

The United States urges Russia to develop an appropriately strong, more transparent, and more effective legal framework and enforcement strategy to reduce the sale of counterfeit goods online and piracy of copyright-protected content. Counterfeit pharmaceuticals are reportedly manufactured in Russia and made available through online pharmacies. The United States notes that Russian courts issued the first two criminal convictions for online piracy this year. Both resulted in suspended sentences, and one also included a fine. It is reported that both cases required investigations of multiple years and that there is little interest in future prosecutions of this type by law enforcement officials. Russia remains home to many sites facilitating online piracy, which damage both the legitimate content market in Russia as well as third-country markets.

Russia has not issued regulations clarifying the protection against the unfair commercial use, as well as unauthorized disclosure, of test and other data generated to obtain marketing approval for pharmaceutical products. Russia has also not enacted a formal review and improvement of its collecting society system, which is nontransparent and burdensome. The United States will continue to monitor Russia's progress on these and other matters.

Algeria

Algeria remains on the Priority Watch List in 2014. The United States welcomes Algeria's intensive work on intellectual property awareness, its accession to the WIPO Internet Treaties, and improved coordination of enforcement agencies and looks forward to seeing tangible results from this work. However, Algeria's ban on a number of imported pharmaceutical products and medical devices in favor of local products is a trade matter of paramount concern, and is the reason Algeria remains on the Priority Watch List. The United States looks forward to continuing its engagement with Algeria, including in the context of Algeria's efforts to accede to the WTO, and urges Algeria to remove this market access barrier.

Argentina

Argentina remains on the Priority Watch List in 2014, a position it has occupied since 1996. Argentina has made little progress in improving protection and enforcement of intellectual property rights over the past year. Significant concerns remain with respect to the high levels of piracy and counterfeiting, including in the digital environment, and the lack of political will to address the situation, although Argentina's customs and tax authority (AFIP) has conducted some enforcement operations. A prime example of the absence of even basic enforcement of IP laws is the continued growth and expansion of the Notorious Market La Salada, and its owners' ability to continue operating with impunity. Delays in the acquisition of IP rights, and a lack of transparency for patentability criteria, also raise concerns. Argentina's patent application backlog is growing, a problem that could be alleviated by Argentina's accession to the Patent Cooperation Treaty (PCT), if the political will to do so existed. Argentina also fails to provide effective protection against unfair commercial use or unauthorized disclosure of test and other data generated to obtain marketing approval for pharmaceutical products. The United States looks forward to continuing to work with Argentina to address these and other issues.

Chile

Chile remains on the Priority Watch List in 2014. The United States continues to have serious concerns regarding outstanding IPR issues under the United States-Chile Free Trade Agreement. The United States continues to urge Chile to implement an effective system for addressing patent issues expeditiously in connection with applications to market pharmaceutical products. The United States also continues to urge Chile to implement both protections against the unlawful circumvention of technological protection measures and protections for encrypted program-carrying satellite signals. Chile must also ensure that effective administrative and judicial procedures, as well as deterrent remedies, are made available to rights holders and satellite and cable service providers, including measures to address ongoing concerns with decoder boxes. The United States also urges Chile to provide adequate protection against unfair commercial use, as well as unauthorized disclosure, of undisclosed test or other data generated to obtain marketing approval for pharmaceutical products. Finally, the United States urges Chile to amend its Internet service provider (ISP) liability regime to permit effective action against piracy over the Internet and to also take steps to improve the protection of plant varieties. The United States looks forward to continuing to work with Chile to resolve these and other issues, including through the TPP negotiations.

Indonesia

Indonesia remains on the Priority Watch List in 2014. Indonesian authorities have continued educational outreach to the public to advance IPR awareness and have engaged with the United States through the IPR Working Group under the United States-Indonesia Trade and Investment Framework Agreement to develop an action plan to improve IPR protection and enforcement to address high levels of IPR infringement in Indonesia. The United States welcomes reports of enforcement raids conducted against counterfeit and pirated goods, as well as a reported increase in actions against counterfeit and substandard pharmaceutical products. However, the United States remains concerned about gaps in Indonesia's laws relating to the protection and enforcement of IPR, and urges Indonesia to address these issues. The United States is also concerned that Indonesia's IPR enforcement efforts, despite the raids mentioned above, have not been effective in addressing rampant piracy and counterfeiting, reflected in growing piracy over the Internet and widely available counterfeit pharmaceutical products. The United States urges Indonesia to take steps to address inefficiencies in its judicial and prosecutorial systems which include a lack of transparency and deterrent-level sentences. In regard to cable piracy, Indonesia has conducted outreach to raise public awareness about unauthorized distribution of cable signals and Indonesia's continuing licensing process. However, these efforts have had little or no impact to date on widespread cable piracy. The United States continues to encourage Indonesia to provide an effective system for protecting against the unfair commercial use, as well as unauthorized disclosure, of undisclosed test or other data generated to obtain marketing approval for pharmaceutical and agricultural chemical products. The United States also remains concerned about market access barriers in Indonesia, including measures that appear to condition permissions to import medicines on at least partial local manufacturing or technology transfer requirements. Other measures that could restrict market access relate to the importation of motion pictures. The United States remains concerned by Indonesian government statements indicating that Indonesia failed to abide by Indonesian legal procedures in issuing a compulsory license decree in 2012, and indicating that Indonesian patent law does not require individual merits review in connection with the grant of compulsory licenses. The United States further encourages Indonesia to provide for judicial or other independent review of any compulsory license authorizations. The United States looks forward to working with Indonesia on these and other matters.

Pakistan

Pakistan remains on the Priority Watch List in 2014. Although Pakistan has continued its efforts to advance IPR enforcement, including through raids, seizures, and arrests by various enforcement authorities, there have not been significant improvements in its overall IPR protection. Pakistan has not yet fully implemented the Intellectual Property Organization of Pakistan Act of 2012 (IPO Act). Notably, Pakistan has yet to establish the specialized IP tribunals and an operational IPO Policy Board provided for under the IPO Act. Widespread counterfeiting and piracy, particularly book and optical disc piracy, continue to present serious concerns for U.S. industry. Pakistan should ensure that its enforcement officials can exercise *ex officio* authority without the need for a formal complaint by a rights holder, and should provide for deterrent-level penalties for criminal IPR infringement. Pakistan should also take the necessary steps to reform its copyright law to address the piracy challenges of the digital age. The United States continues to encourage Pakistan to provide an effective system for protecting against unfair commercial use, as well as unauthorized disclosure, of tests and other data generated to obtain marketing approval for pharmaceutical products. The United States appreciates Pakistan's interest in improving its IPR environment and looks forward to working with Pakistan to address these and other issues, including in connection with Pakistan's implementation of the IPO Act.

Thailand

Thailand remains on the Priority Watch List in 2014. The United States remains encouraged by Thailand's stated commitment to improving IPR protection and enforcement, and is hopeful that the National IPR Center of Enforcement, launched in March 2013, will help to improve coordination and allow for more effective enforcement actions among Thai enforcement agencies. The United States urges Thailand to complete many of the legislative initiatives begun in past years, including: legislation to address landlord liability and unauthorized camcording of motion pictures in theaters; to provide Thai Customs with *ex officio* authority; to fully implement the provisions of the WIPO Internet Treaties; to restructure the Trade Secret Committee and modify penalty provisions under the Trade Secrets Act; to accelerate patent examination and registration procedures and address issues such as partial designs; and to establish improved legal mechanisms to address the rapidly growing problem of copyright piracy and trademark counterfeiting on the Internet. The United States also urges Thailand to take enforcement action against widespread piracy and counterfeiting in the country; to impose deterrent-level sentences; and to address effectively its longstanding problem of piracy of cable and satellite signals. The United States continues to encourage Thailand to provide an effective system for protecting against the unfair commercial use, as well as unauthorized disclosure, of test or other data generated to obtain marketing approval for pharmaceutical and agricultural chemical products. The United States urges Thailand to engage in a meaningful and transparent manner with all relevant stakeholders, including IPR owners, as it considers ways to address Thailand's public health challenges, while maintaining a patent system that promotes innovation. The United States looks forward to continuing to work with Thailand to address these and other issues.

Venezuela

Venezuela remains on the Priority Watch List in 2014. Issues of continuing concern include: questions about the consistency of domestic laws and international obligations resulting from the 2008 reinstatement of the 1955 Industrial Property Law; the status of trademarks that were registered under the Andean Community law prior to Venezuela's withdrawal from the Andean Community; and lack of enforcement against counterfeiting and piracy, both physical and online. The United States also continues to encourage Venezuela to provide an effective system for protecting against the unfair commercial use, as well as unauthorized disclosure, of undisclosed test or other data generated to obtain marketing approval for pharmaceutical products.

WATCH LIST

Barbados

Barbados remains on the Watch List in 2014. The United States continues to be concerned in Barbados and throughout the Caribbean region about the interception and retransmission of United States cable programming by local cable operators without the consent of, and without adequately compensating, United States rights holders. The United States also continues to have concerns in Barbados and throughout the region about the refusal of local TV and radio broadcasters and cable/satellite operators to pay for public performances of music. (*See* Section I). The United States urges the Government of Barbados to take all administrative actions necessary, without undue delay, to ensure that all composers and songwriters receive the royalties they are owed for the public performance of their musical works. In addition, the United States urges the Government of Barbados to adopt copyright legislation that protects works in both the physical and online environments and to take steps to prevent the unauthorized and uncompensated retransmission of copyrighted musical and audiovisual content. The United States looks forward to working with Barbados to resolve these and other issues.

Belarus

Belarus remains on the Watch List in 2014. Despite recent efforts to improve enforcement against IP infringements, including methods for collecting and preserving evidence of IPR violations involving the Internet, piracy and counterfeiting remain widespread. Belarus has still not passed amendments to the Criminal, Administrative and Procedural codes originally proposed in 2011, and has not yet established civil remedies or criminal penalties for online piracy. The United States appreciates the government's decision to approve the Eurasian Economic Commission Board's agreement on coordination of measures to protect IPR and encourages Belarus to further harmonize its IPR regime with the regulatory principles adopted under the Customs Union. For example, Belarus could improve the investigation of suspected infringement cases, seizure of infringing goods, and prosecution of IPR violations by creating the unified trademark registry and implementing and exercising the *ex officio* authority provisions of the Customs Union Customs Code. The United States appreciates recent outreach by Belarus on IPR matters and looks forward to working with Belarus on these and other issues.

Bolivia

Bolivia remains on the Watch List in 2014. The Government of Bolivia has undertaken public awareness efforts and has made some enforcement attempts, but rampant piracy and counterfeiting persist. The United States encourages Bolivia to take steps to improve its enforcement of IPR, including by improving coordination among Bolivian enforcement authorities and with the authorities of its neighboring countries.

Brazil

Brazil remains on the Watch List in 2014. Brazil continues on a generally positive trajectory regarding both its domestic intellectual property rights (IPR) policy and its enforcement of IPR. Brazil has taken steps to address a backlog of pending patent and trademark applications, including by authorizing the hiring of for new examiners, but very long delays still exist. Brazil has also continued to make progress in enhancing the effectiveness of IPR enforcement, conducting raids across the country under the coordination of the National Council to Combat Piracy. Significant concerns remain with respect to the high levels of counterfeiting and piracy, including Internet piracy; however, positive strides have been made in the area of pay-television piracy. Although laudable enforcement efforts also have occurred at the border, greater emphasis on this challenge is needed, particularly in the tri-border region, including the issuance of more deterrent penalties in such cases. Concerns also persist with respect to Brazil's inadequate protection against unfair commercial use of undisclosed test and other data generated to obtain marketing approval for pharmaceutical products. In addition, regulations that provide Brazil's health authority, the National Sanitary Regulatory Agency (ANVISA), with the authority to review pharmaceutical patent applications for patentability requirements are not transparent or predictable and appear to contravene earlier opinions by the Federal Attorney General, which clarified that ANVISA does not have such authority. The United States is also concerned about a series of lawsuits recently filed by Brazil's National Industrial Property Institute (INPI) seeking to invalidate or shorten the term of certain "mailbox" patents for pharmaceutical and agrochemical products. The United States believes it is important for Brazil to continue to create an IP climate that affords both domestic and foreign IP holders with incentives to invest in the market. We look forward to engaging constructively with Brazil in support of its work in the IPR arena and to address remaining concerns.

Bulgaria

Bulgaria is on the Watch List in 2014. Despite some limited improvements, the United States continues to have serious concerns regarding IPR infringement in Bulgaria. Copyright piracy over the Internet in Bulgaria remains a significant problem in this market. Numerous online infringing services operate in the market and enforcement actions seldom result in convictions or deterrent sentences. Investigations on copyright piracy, including against enterprise end-user software piracy, initiated by the Bulgarian anti-cybercrime unit have stalled because that unit's responsibilities and personnel were transferred to a different agency. The number of working sessions of the Council for IPR Protection have declined and there are fewer staff in the Copyright Office of the Ministry of Culture, twin events that have weakened Bulgaria's ability to effectively enforce its IP laws. Collecting societies continue to report serious challenges in collecting royalties and in enforcing their rights through administrative or judicial actions. High levels of trademark counterfeiting also persist. The government has reduced staffing at the Patent Office, which is responsible for registrations (e.g., patents and trademarks) as well as certain enforcement functions (e.g., inspections, issuance of fines, and sentencing in cases referred from criminal courts), thereby hindering that office's ability to make sufficient routine inspections or to conduct adequate enforcement. Bad faith trademark applications are also a growing concern and are often granted due to these constraints at the Bulgarian Patent Office. Unfortunately, a lack of coordination between investigation and prosecution authorities creates inefficiencies in the effective enforcement of IP cases, which is compounded by inadequacies in the Bulgarian judicial system. Generally, rights holders face significant delays in the adjudication of IPR disputes, many of which do not reach final sentencing, and when they do, remedies are not a deterrent to further infringements. Bulgaria's government should coordinate with rights holders and other interested parties, such as Internet service providers (ISPs), to develop recommendations for reducing Internet piracy. We also encourage Bulgaria to engage in meaningful follow-up on its Mass Software Compliance Campaign initiated by the Ministries of Culture and Interior in early 2013. Notwithstanding these continuing issues, the United States recognizes the positive steps Bulgaria has taken to address IPR infringement in its market. For example, Bulgaria has been able to engage in certain enforcement actions, including those led by the Ministry of Culture. The Ministry of Culture's Copyright Office also facilitated a royalty payment agreement between the holders of film rights and the Bulgarian Association of Cable and Communication Operators (BACCO). The United States encourages Bulgaria to continue to enhance its IPR protection and enforcement efforts and intensify its engagement on IPR public awareness. The United States looks forward to continuing to work with Bulgaria to address these and other issues.

Canada

Canada remains on the Watch List in 2014. On copyright issues, the United States welcomed the passage of the Copyright Modernization Act in June 2012. As part of Canada's implementation of this law, the United States urges Canada to implement its WIPO Internet Treaties commitments in a manner consistent with its international obligations and to continue to address the challenges of copyright piracy in the digital age. Regarding border enforcement issues, Canada re-introduced the Combating Counterfeit Products Act in October 2013 to strengthen IPR enforcement. The bill included provisions that would provide *ex officio* authority to Canadian customs officials to seize pirated and counterfeit goods at the border. The United States supports Canada's commitment to address the serious problem of pirated and counterfeit goods entering our highly integrated supply chains and urges Canada, as it proceeds with this legislation, to expand its scope to provide authority for its customs officials to take action against such goods in-transit. With respect to pharmaceuticals, the United States continues to have serious concerns about the availability of rights of appeal in Canada's administrative process for reviewing regulatory approval of pharmaceutical products. The United States also has serious concerns about the lack of clarity and the impact of the heightened utility requirements for patents that Canadian courts have applied recently. Under this amorphous and evolving standard, courts can invalidate a patent on utility grounds by construing the "promise of a patent" years after the patent has been granted, leading to uncertainty for patent holders and applicants and undermining incentives for investment in the pharmaceutical sector. In applying this standard, courts have invalidated a number of patents held by U.S. pharmaceutical companies, finding now that those products lack utility (*i.e.*, not capable of industrial application), even though such products have been in the market and benefiting patients for years. The United

States will closely monitor developments on these issues and looks forward to continuing to work with Canada to address these and other IPR issues, including through the TPP negotiations.

Colombia

Colombia remains on the Watch List in 2014. The Government of Colombia has made tangible progress in the areas of internal coordination of enforcement agencies, reducing patent application backlogs, and training judges and law enforcement officials on IPR issues. However, earlier progress on IPR legislation was reversed in 2013 when the Colombian Constitutional Court invalidated on procedural grounds the law enacting many IPR-related commitments made under the United States-Colombia Trade Promotion Agreement (CTPA). Colombia has not yet reestablished the provisions contained in the earlier invalidated law. In addition, Colombia's limitations on the patentability of certain pharmaceuticals and challenges related to pharmaceutical and agrochemical data protection are areas of concern. The United States urges Colombia to implement geographical indications protections in a manner that is consistent with its obligations under the CTPA. Persistently high levels of both hard goods and Internet piracy continue to plague the country in spite of periodic, laudable enforcement efforts. For example, Colombia's San Andresitos markets remain rife with counterfeit and pirated products and were again named in USTR's Notorious Markets List in 2013. Greater enforcement attention is needed to disrupt organized distribution of illicit goods, including in the border areas. The United States looks forward to continuing constructive engagement with Colombia on these and other matters.

Costa Rica

Costa Rica remains on the Watch List in 2014. Costa Rica's efforts to address certain longstanding problems have not yet taken hold and new problems have arisen in the meantime. Several long-term concerns relate to weak IPR enforcement. Few criminal prosecutions result in deterrent-level sentencing in Costa Rica, despite growing evidence of links between certain IPR infringement and organized crime. The United States applauded a 2011 announcement that a specialized IPR prosecution unit would be created, but it is unclear whether that initiative is actually underway. Similarly, while the government of Costa Rica announced a plan in 2010 to ensure that the government would use only licensed software, progress has been limited until recently, and actual results remain unknown. Costa Rican law still allows Internet service providers (ISPs) 45 days to forward infringement notices to subscribers, which represents a very long period of time, especially considering that certain content may be of relatively short-term interest to the public. Pharmaceutical patent holders report a number of concerns, including poorly defined exceptions to Costa Rica's data exclusivity regime. The United States encourages Costa Rica to engage with the private sector and other interested parties as it evaluates legislative reforms relating to health care. In terms of new problems, initial administrative determinations on applications to register certain geographical indications present a notable concern, as first-level authorities seemed not to acknowledge relevant evidence presented by interested parties in opposition. At the same time, Costa Rica has taken positive steps forward. Costa Rica has rolled out an electronically searchable trademark database, it has compiled better enforcement statistics, and it has formed and trained a new border police unit, which could have a positive impact on IPR enforcement. Given Costa Rica's demonstrated ability to address issues of its choosing, the United States urges Costa Rica to develop clear plans to tackle longstanding problems and to demonstrate tangible progress in implementing those plans prior to the next Special 301 review.

Dominican Republic

The Dominican Republic remains on the Watch List in 2014. While several positive developments merit recognition, substantial concerns remain, especially with respect to the widespread availability of pirated and counterfeit products. In terms of steps forward, Dominican Republic authorities have provided more effective regulatory protection against pharmaceutical patent infringement and have in individual cases provided for the protection of undisclosed test and other data generated to obtain marketing approval for pharmaceutical products against unfair commercial use and unauthorized disclosure, although the United States urges the Dominican Republic to clarify the governing procedural frameworks. The Dominican Republic has also made a trademark database available online. Nevertheless, IPR enforcement agencies in the Dominican Republic continue to experience a lack of coordination, resources, and training. As an example, the Dominican Republic reports enhanced enforcement efforts to address cable signal piracy, yet the private sector has not observed a substantial resulting impact. A major and unresolved problem is the Dominican Republic's large backlog of pending patent applications. Over 1,300 patent applications were pending as of January 2014, whereas less than 250 patent certificates were issued from 2000-2013. The multi-year delays in the patent application and examination process highlight the urgent need to reduce the backlog and to address outstanding concerns to implement CAFTA-DR obligations with respect to patent term adjustment. The United States looks forward to continuing to work with the Dominican Republic to address these and other issues.

Ecuador

Ecuador remains on the Watch List in 2014. The United States is very concerned about the recent de-criminalization of IPR infringement. Ecuador continues to experience high levels of piracy and counterfeiting and relatively low levels of enforcement. The repeal of the criminal enforcement provisions will only exacerbate the situation. On a positive note, Ecuador's Institute for Intellectual Property (IEPI) has undertaken public awareness efforts to attempt to address the rampant IP theft occurring in Ecuador, including at La Bahia, a 2013 Notorious Market. However, the United States remains concerned about the institutional weakening of IEPI under a 2012 government reorganization. Furthermore, IEPI's 2012 enactment of exorbitant fees for patent and plant variety registration and maintenance, and the lack of protection against unfair commercial use, as well as unauthorized disclosure, of undisclosed test or other data generated to obtain marketing approval for pharmaceutical and agricultural chemical products could have an adverse effect on foreign investment in those sectors.

Egypt

Egypt remains on the Watch List in 2014. IPR challenges for Egypt include the failure to obtain deterrent-level sentences for IPR violations that are prosecuted and the need for additional training for enforcement officials. Egypt has not issued regulations to clarify border procedures for the destruction of counterfeit and pirated products and to provide customs officials with the authority to take *ex officio* action. The United States urges Egypt to clarify its protection against the unfair commercial use, as well as unauthorized disclosure, of undisclosed test or other data generated to obtain marketing approval of pharmaceutical products. Although Egypt is working to upgrade its trademark system, rights holders have expressed concerns about the registration of trademarks filed in bad-faith. Rights holders have reported certain market access impediments, such as fees and taxes applied to foreign films. The United States appreciates Egypt's recent engagement on many of these and other IPR issues and stands ready to work with Egypt to improve its IPR regime.

Finland

Finland remains on the Watch List in 2014. The United States continues to be concerned about the lack of product patent protection for certain pharmaceutical products. U.S. industry also has expressed concern that the regulatory framework in Finland regarding process patents filed before 1995, and pending in 1996, denies adequate protection to many of the top-selling U.S. pharmaceutical products currently on the Finnish market. The United States looks forward to continuing to work with Finland to address these and other issues.

Greece

Greece remains on the Watch List in 2014. U.S. concerns continue with respect to several IPR protection and enforcement issues in Greece. The United States encourages Greece to continue its efforts to implement the 2009 IPR Action Plan, which identifies many of these priority issues. Greece should fully implement legislation and regulations that provide administrative fines for software infringement. Greece should also take steps to ensure that it has effective legal mechanisms to address piracy over the Internet, including by implementing existing measures that allow civil actions by rights holders concerning piracy over the Internet, as well as by providing ISPs with clear incentives to cooperate with rights holders in removing unauthorized content. The lack of adequate governmental resources to combat piracy over the Internet has exacerbated this growing problem. In addition, Greece should expand on its enforcement efforts to address the continuing widespread availability of pirated and counterfeit goods. The United States also continues to encourage Greece to address key challenges facing IPR enforcement in the Greek judicial system, including significant delays and few infringement convictions. Greece has made progress, however, in a few key areas. There has been positive development in trademark protection particularly by passing a new trademark law which established the Illegal Trade Coordination Center (SYKAP). Moreover, national police, customs, and financial police also conducted investigations which resulted in seizures of counterfeit and pirated goods. In particular, rights holders have experienced excellent cooperation with the Tax Police in addressing enterprise end-user software piracy. The United States looks forward to continuing to work with Greece to address these and other issues.

Guatemala

Guatemala remains on the Watch List in 2014. While a number of problems remain outstanding, the United States applauds the Government of Guatemala's willingness to consider U.S. perspectives and concerns as Guatemala amended its laws and regulations relating to protections for geographical indications. Administrative authorities in Guatemala recently issued rulings on applications to register geographical indications (GIs) that appear sound and well-reasoned for compound GI names, but U.S. exporters remain concerned that rulings on single-name GIs, particularly related to dairy products, may prohibit new marketing opportunities for those products in Guatemala. On another positive note, enforcement activity increased in 2013 as compared to 2012, although it remained relatively ineffective given the scale of IPR infringement in Guatemala. Pirated and counterfeit goods continue to be widely available in Guatemala, and enforcement efforts are hampered by limited resources and the need for better coordination among all enforcement agencies. Trademark squatting is a significant concern, as administrative remedies are inadequate and relief through the courts is slow and expensive. Government use of unlicensed software is another problem that remains largely unaddressed. While the United States was encouraged by the 2011 enactment of legislation to strengthen penalties against the production and distribution of counterfeit medicines, and some enforcement efforts were initiated very recently, the United States is not aware of any successful prosecutions under the law. The United States urges Guatemala to engage with private industry and other interested parties regarding the protection and enforcement of intellectual property rights for pharmaceutical products and related legislative initiatives. The United States encourages Guatemala to sustain and further increase its enforcement efforts against the manufacture of pirated and counterfeit goods, and to take steps to improve the operation of its judicial system. The United States looks forward to continuing to work with Guatemala to address these and other matters.

Jamaica

Jamaica remains on the Watch List in 2014. The United States continues to encourage Jamaica to pass the long-awaited Patent and Designs Act. In the area of copyright, Jamaica is one of several Caribbean countries with deficiencies related to protection and enforcement. (*See* Section I). For several years, Jamaica has been identified by rights holders as one of the region's most problematic markets with respect to the unlicensed and uncompensated cable-casting and broadcasting of copyrighted music. Jamaica has taken steps to ensure its regulatory agencies are monitoring broadcasting entities and has pledged an open door policy to rights holders to discuss their specific IP-related concerns. However, Jamaica maintains a statutory licensing regime for the retransmission of copyrighted television programming but has not consistently enforced the payment of statutory royalties to rights holders. The United States looks forward to continuing to work with Jamaica to address these and other issues.

Kuwait

Although Kuwait remains on the Watch List, the United States will conduct an Out-of-Cycle Review (OCR) in September 2014 to determine whether to elevate Kuwait to the Priority Watch List. The review is prompted both by Kuwait's failure for more than 14 years to draft and pass amendments to its copyright law to meet international standards, and the recent sharp decline in enforcement actions against copyright and trademark infringement. If Kuwait does not introduce to the National Assembly legislation which will result in a copyright law that is consistent with international standards and does not resume enforcement against copyright and trademark infringement by the time of the OCR, Kuwait will be moved to the Priority Watch List. The United States notes that the Kuwait Customs IPR Office has not halted its IP enforcement efforts, and commends the work by that office. The United States remains willing to work with Kuwait on these important issues.

Lebanon

Lebanon remains on the Watch List in 2014. The United States continues to encourage Lebanon to make progress on pending IPR legislative reforms, including amendments to Lebanon's patent and copyright laws and efforts to accede to the WIPO Internet treaties. The United States encourages the Parliament to approve several additional IPR treaties that have been forwarded by the Cabinet, including the Paris Convention for the Protection of Industrial Property, the Berne Convention for the Protection of Literary and Artistic Works, the Singapore Treaty on the Law of Trademarks, and the Patent Cooperation Treaty. Additionally, the United States encourages Lebanon to provide its Cyber Crime and Intellectual Property Rights Bureau (CCIPRB) with *ex officio* enforcement authority as well as to provide all of its enforcement authorities with adequate resources to carry out their enforcement functions. The United States looks forward to continuing to work with Lebanon to address these and other issues.

Mexico

Mexico remains on the Watch List in 2014. Positive developments in Mexico in 2013 included entry into force of the Madrid Protocol, implementation of amendments to the copyright law that allow rights holders to seek damages in civil courts before an administrative infringement decision is issued or becomes final, and progress in the destruction of seized illegal goods, although overall seizure numbers have declined. However, serious concerns remain, particularly with respect to the widespread availability of pirated and counterfeit goods in Mexico, including at the Notorious Markets Tepito and San Juan de Dios, and also increased Internet piracy due in part to higher broadband penetration. Although coordination has been increasing, criminal enforcement suffers from inefficient coordination among federal and sub-federal officials, as well as a lack of resources. In addition, to combat high levels of IPR infringement, Mexico needs to devote additional resources, bring more IPR-related prosecutions, and impose deterrent penalties against infringers. The United States continues to urge Mexico to provide its customs officials with *ex officio* authority and to enact legislation to strengthen its copyright regime, including by fully implementing the WIPO Internet Treaties and providing stronger protection against the unauthorized camcording of motion pictures in theaters. Prior to 2011, Mexican customs authorities and the Attorney General's Office worked jointly to intercept and prosecute transshipments of counterfeit and pirated goods. Following a shift in policy, however, Mexican authorities now only take action against transshipments of suspected infringing goods if there is evidence of "intent for commercial gain" in Mexican territory, which is very difficult to prove. The United States strongly urges Mexico to revert to the previous policy that allowed for the interception of potentially dangerous counterfeit trademark goods in transit to the United States and other countries. The United States looks forward to continuing to work with Mexico to address these and other issues, including through the TPP negotiations.

Paraguay

Paraguay remains on the Watch List in 2014. In addition, the United States continues to monitor Paraguay under Section 306. The Government of Paraguay has taken positive steps toward strengthening IPR, particularly since President Cartes took office in August 2013. On October 10, 2013, President Cartes signed the implementing regulation (Decree 460) for Law 4798 of 2012 that created the National Directorate of Intellectual Property (DINAPI). DINAPI is now the Paraguayan government authority responsible for the issuance and protection of copyrights, trademarks, patents, industrial designs, and geographical indications. Additionally, the law authorizes DINAPI's enforcement arm, the General Enforcement Directorate, to conduct administrative investigations and initiate proceedings at customs checkpoints and businesses. Decree 460 also mandates the creation of a National IPR Policy, which has yet to be drafted. In December 2013, DINAPI granted pharmaceutical patents to two U.S. companies, the first patents reportedly granted since 2005. DINAPI has also undertaken outreach to the public, signed inter-institutional cooperative agreements to improve IPR protection and enforcement, and has stepped up enforcement operations, including at the border. The United States looks forward to working constructively with Paraguay to address enforcement and other challenges, and to conclude negotiations re-launched in March 2014 on a bilateral IPR Memorandum of Understanding (MOU). Upon successful conclusion of the MOU, USTR will initiate an Out-of-Cycle Review to remove Paraguay from the Watch List.

Peru

Peru remains on the Watch List in 2014. The United States remains concerned about the widespread availability of counterfeit and pirated products in Peru. The United States urges Peru to devote additional resources for IPR enforcement, improve coordination among enforcement agencies, enhance its border controls, and strengthen its judicial system. The United States encourages Peru to coordinate enforcement and pursue prosecutions under the law that criminalizes the sale of counterfeit medicines. In addition, the United States urges Peru to take steps to implement its obligations under the United States-Peru Trade Promotion Agreement regarding the prevention of government use of unlicensed software, and likewise urges steps to implement obligations with respect to protections against piracy over the Internet, which continues to be a growing problem. Peru also needs to clarify its protections for biotechnologically-derived pharmaceutical products. The United States looks forward to continuing to work with Peru to address these and other issues, including through the TPP negotiations.

Romania

Romania remains on the Watch List in 2014. Despite positive instances of collaboration between the Romanian government and stakeholders, systemic concerns remain with respect to IPR protection and enforcement in that market. The United States encourages Romania to prioritize IPR protection and enforcement and urges Romania to devote the necessary resources and training for authorities to effectively address the continuing problems of piracy and counterfeiting. In 2013, for example, the number of enforcement actions taken dropped significantly when compared to 2012. Additionally, the General Prosecutor's IPR coordination department lacks sufficient staff. Romania should also take steps to address concerns over judicial delays and a lack of deterrent-level sentencing. Piracy over the Internet remains a serious concern, and more enforcement efforts are needed to address the problem. While some concerns persist, Romania has taken some positive steps. For example, cooperation between law enforcement, prosecutors, and IP-based industry groups continues to be close and effective at the working level. Notably, the GPO IPR Department also drafted guidelines for conducting Internet piracy investigations, and issued new procedures for prosecuting IPR crimes, which came into force on January 1, 2014. Notably, these procedures have resulted in positive enforcement actions against online piracy and counterfeiting. The United States looks forward to continuing to work with Romania to address these and other issues.

Tajikistan

Tajikistan remains on the Watch List in 2014. The United States urges Tajikistan to implement fully amendments of its Customs Code to provide *ex officio* authority to its customs and criminal enforcement officials, as discussed in connection with Tajikistan's WTO accession. The United States continues to recommend that Tajikistan increase prosecutions of criminal IPR infringement, and address optical disc piracy as well as reports of government use of unlicensed software. The United States looks forward to continuing to work with Tajikistan to increase its enforcement capacity in general, and to advance Tajikistan's implementation of commitments made as part of Tajikistan's WTO accession process.

Trinidad and Tobago

Trinidad and Tobago remains on the Watch List in 2014. The United States continues to urge the Government of Trinidad and Tobago to enforce the copyright provisions of its cable license agreements against cable operators who refuse to negotiate with the Copyright Music Organization of Trinidad and Tobago ("COTT"), the local performing rights organization, for compensation for public performance of music, including for music written by American composers. Particularly troubling is the situation with local cable operator FLOW. A court in 2011 found that FLOW is required to obtain a public performance license from and pay all applicable fees to COTT. However, nearly three years later, judicial authorities have not completed the appeal hearing nor assessed royalties owed to COTT. Furthermore, notwithstanding this decision, the local cable operator has failed to obtain the required public performance license, in violation of its cable license agreement with the government. The United States urges the Government of Trinidad and Tobago to take all necessary actions to ensure that the terms of such licenses be fulfilled or that those licenses be terminated. The United States also urges the Government of Trinidad and Tobago to address optical media piracy and other forms of IPR infringement. These issues affect not only American artists but Caribbean artists as well. The United States looks forward to continuing to work with Trinidad and Tobago to address these and other issues.

Turkey

Turkey remains on the Watch List in 2014. U.S. rights holders continue to raise serious concerns regarding the export from, and transshipment through, Turkey of counterfeit and pirated products. In particular, industry has expressed concern about the manufacture of counterfeited luxury goods, digital media, and textiles. Software piracy is also a growing problem. Serial code crackers and key generators used to gain unlawful access to software are commonly available, and in some cases, computers sold at retail stores are preloaded with illegal software. Legislative proposals intended to improve copyright and industrial property protections have not yet been finalized and passed. Adequate, transparent, and effective enforcement of IPR remains a significant challenge in Turkey, including due to obstacles posed by judicial delays, rarity of deterrent-level penalties, and the fact that the Turkish National Police lack *ex officio* authority. However, the United States congratulates Turkey on several successful enforcement initiatives resulting in the prosecution of individuals selling counterfeit medicines online and the seizure of printing presses and materials used to counterfeit pharmaceutical packaging, as well as the seizure of pirated books, counterfeited food products, and counterfeited cancer treatments. In addition, the United States notes that the Turkish National Police, Turkish Patent Institute, and Ministry of Culture and Tourism, as well as other agencies in the Turkish government, participated in several training, coordination, and public education initiatives, and the United States looks forward to seeing this productive cooperation between Turkey, WIPO, the United States, INTERPOL, and others continue. The United States looks forward to working with Turkey on these and other issues.

Turkmenistan

Turkmenistan remains on the Watch List in 2014. In 2012, Turkmenistan adopted a Law on Copyright and Allied Rights and amended its Civil Code to enhance IPR protection. However, Turkmenistan reportedly has yet to provide for effective administrative, civil or criminal procedures or penalties for enforcement of these rights. The United States urges Turkmenistan to provide for such enforcement procedures, including but not limited to *ex officio* authority for its customs officials. In addition, the United States continues to strongly encourage Turkmenistan to join the Berne Convention on the Protection of Literary and Artistic Works and the Convention for the Protection of Producers of Phonograms Against Unauthorized

Duplication of their Phonographs (Geneva Phonograms Convention). The United States looks forward to continuing to work with Turkmenistan on these and other issues.

Uzbekistan

Uzbekistan remains on the Watch List in 2014. The United States congratulates Uzbekistan on the long-awaited passage of legislation that resulted in withdrawal of Uzbekistan's reservation to Article 18 of the Berne Convention for the Protection of Literary and Artistic Works, which relates to the protection of works created before 2005. However, the Uzbekistani Parliament should immediately take several legislative steps to address longstanding deficiencies in IPR protection. Specifically, it should: (1) approve Uzbekistan joining the Convention for the Protection of Producers of Phonograms Against Unauthorized Duplication of their Phonographs (Geneva Phonograms Convention); (2) approve Uzbekistan's accession to the WIPO Copyright Treaty and WIPO Performances and Phonograms Treaty (WIPO Internet Treaties); and (3) take legislative action to provide adequate copyright protection for foreign sound recordings. Additionally, Uzbekistan should provide additional resources to the Agency for Intellectual Property and other enforcement agencies as well as *ex officio* authority to initiate investigations and enforcement actions, including at the border. Uzbekistan also lacks deterrent-level penalties for IPR infringement. The United States will continue to engage with Uzbekistan on these IPR matters.

Vietnam

Vietnam remains on the Watch List in 2014. Although Vietnam took certain steps to improve its regulatory framework in 2012 and 2013 by passing decrees and issuing circulars to strengthen copyright protection and enforcement, significant areas of concern remain. Piracy and sales of counterfeit goods over the Internet are a growing concern, and counterfeit goods also remain widely available in physical markets. In addition, book piracy, software piracy (including on government computer systems), and cable and satellite signal theft continue to be widespread. Although Vietnam took further steps to improve public awareness efforts, Vietnam has made little progress in advancing enforcement actions. Enforcement agencies continue to have capacity constraints, due in part to a lack of resources and IPR expertise, and the lack of coordination among the agencies with enforcement jurisdiction is a further complicating factor. Vietnam should clarify its system for protecting against the unfair commercial use, as well as unauthorized disclosure, of undisclosed test or other data generated to obtain marketing approval for pharmaceutical products. While Vietnam has broad laws criminalizing IPR crimes, the government has yet to draft the implementing guidelines that are necessary for law enforcement agencies and the courts to levy deterrent criminal penalties against IPR violators. The United States looks forward to continuing to work with Vietnam to address these and other issues, including in the TPP negotiations.

ANNEX 1. SPECIAL 301 STATUTORY BASIS

Special 301 Statutory Authority

Pursuant to the Special 301 statutory mandate, Section 182 of the Trade Act of 1974, as amended by the Omnibus Trade and Competitiveness Act of 1988 and the Uruguay Round Agreements Act of 1994 (19 U.S.C. § 2242), USTR is required to identify "those foreign countries that deny adequate and effective protection of intellectual property rights, or deny fair and equitable market access to United States persons that rely upon intellectual property protection." The USTR shall only designate countries that have the most onerous or egregious acts, policies, or practices and whose acts, policies, or practices have the greatest adverse impact (actual or potential) on the relevant U.S. products as Priority Foreign Countries. Priority Foreign Countries are potentially subject to an investigation under the Section 301 provisions of the Trade Act of 1974. USTR may not designate a country as a Priority Foreign Country if it is entering into good faith negotiations or making significant progress in bilateral or multilateral negotiations to provide adequate and effective protection of IPR. USTR is required to decide whether to identify countries within 30 days after issuance of the annual National Trade Estimate Report. In addition, USTR may identify a trading partner as a Priority Foreign Country or re-designate the trading partner whenever warranted.

USTR has created a Priority Watch List and Watch List under the Special 301 provisions. Placement of a trading partner on the Priority Watch List or Watch List indicates that particular problems exist in that country with respect to IPR protection, enforcement, or market access for persons relying on IPR. Countries placed on the Priority Watch List are the focus of increased bilateral attention concerning the problem areas.

Additionally, under Section 306, USTR monitors a trading partner's compliance with measures that are the basis for resolving an investigation under Section 301. USTR may apply sanctions if a country fails to satisfactorily implement such measures.

The Trade Policy Staff Committee, in particular the Special 301 Subcommittee, in advising USTR on the implementation of Special 301, obtains information from and holds consultations with the private sector, U.S. embassies, foreign governments, and the U.S. Congress, among other sources.

ANNEX 2. UNITED STATES GOVERNMENT-SPONSORED TECHNICAL ASSISTANCE AND CAPACITY BUILDING

In addition to identifying concerns, this Report also highlights opportunities for the U.S. Government to work closely with trading partners to address those concerns. The U.S. Government collaborates with various trading partners on IPR-related training and capacity building around the world. Domestically and abroad, bilaterally, and in regional groupings, the U.S. Government remains engaged in building stronger, more streamlined, and more effective systems for the protection and enforcement of IPR.

Although many trading partners have enacted IPR legislation, a lack of criminal prosecutions and deterrent sentencing has reduced the effectiveness of IPR enforcement in many regions. These problems result from several factors, including a lack of knowledge of IPR law on the part of judges and enforcement officials, and insufficient enforcement resources. The United States welcomes steps by a number of trading partners to educate their judiciary and enforcement officials on IPR matters. The United States will continue to work collaboratively with trading partners to address these issues.

The U.S. Patent and Trademark Office (USPTO), through the Global Intellectual Property Academy (GIPA) and the Office of Policy and International Affairs offers programs in the United States and around the world to provide education, training, and capacity building on IPR protection, commercialization, and enforcement. These programs are offered to patent, trademark, and copyright officials, judges and prosecutors, police and customs officials, foreign policy makers, and U.S. rights holders.

Other U.S. Government agencies bring foreign government and private sector representatives to the United States on study tours to meet with IPR professionals and to visit the institutions and businesses responsible for developing, protecting, and promoting IPR in the United States. One such program is the Department of State's International Visitors Leadership Program, which brings groups from around the world to cities across the United States to learn more about IPR and related trade and business issues.

Overseas, the U.S. Government is also active in partnering to provide training, technical assistance, capacity building, exchange of best practices, and other collaborative activities to improve IPR protection and enforcement. The following are examples of these programs.

- In 2013, GIPA provided training to 7,078 foreign IPR officials from 135 countries, through 114 separate programs. Attendees included IPR policy makers, judges, prosecutors, customs officers, and examiners, and training topics covered the entire spectrum of IPR. Post-training surveys demonstrated that 100 percent of all attendees reported that they had taken some steps to implement positive policy change in their respective organizations.

- GIPA also has produced seven free distance-learning modules, available on its website in multiple languages (English, Spanish, French, Arabic, and Russian). There have been over 41,460 hits on those modules since being placed on the USPTO.gov site in early 2010.

- In addition, the USPTO's Office of Policy and International Affairs provides capacity building in countries around the world, and has concluded agreements with 20 national, regional, and international IPR organizations, such as the United Kingdom Intellectual Property Office (UKIPO), Japan Patent Office (JPO), European Patent Office (EPO), German Patent and Trademark Office (DPMA), Government Agencies of the People's Republic of China, Mexican Institute of Industrial Property (IMPI), the Korean Intellectual Property Office (KIPO), and the World Intellectual Property Organization (WIPO). These partnerships help establish a framework for joint development of informational, educational IP content, technical cooperation, and classification activities.

- The Department of Commerce's International Trade Administration (ITA) collaborates with the private sector to develop programs to heighten the awareness of the dangers of counterfeit products and of the economic value of IPR to national economies. Additionally, ITA develops and shares small business tools to help domestic and foreign businesses understand IPR. ITA, working closely with other U.S. Government agencies and foreign partners, developed and made available IPR training materials in English, Spanish, and French. Under the auspices of the Transatlantic IPR Working Group, ITA worked closely with the European Union's Directorate General for Enterprise and Industry to establish a Transatlantic IPR Portal so the resources of our respective governments are quickly and easily accessible to the public. All of the ITA-developed resources, including the Transatlantic IPR Portal, as well as information and links to the other programs identified in this Annex, are accessible via www.STOPfakes.gov.

- In 2013, the U.S. Immigration and Customs Enforcement (ICE) Homeland Security Investigations (HSI), through the National IPR Coordination Center (IPR Center) and in conjunction with INTERPOL, conducted law enforcement training programs in India, Mexico, Morocco, Algeria, Botswana, Zambia, Namibia, Malawi, Singapore and Thailand, and in France for countries from Southeast Asia. ICE-HSI trained officials and police officers from Mexico, India, Indonesia, Thailand, Vietnam, China, Fiji, Singapore, Algeria, Morocco, Botswana, Malawi, South Africa, Zambia, and Zimbabwe. The IPR Center also conducted advanced training programs at the International Law Enforcement Academies (ILEAs) in Botswana, El Salvador, Hungary, and Peru for participants from 26 countries.

- The Department of State provides training funds each year to U.S. Government agencies that provide IPR enforcement training and technical assistance to foreign governments. The agencies that provide such training include the U.S. Department of Justice (DOJ), USPTO, U.S. Customs and Border Protection (CBP), and ICE. In 2013, the Department of State provided funds for 18 training programs for customs, police, and judicial officials from various trading partners, including Pakistan, Mexico, Indonesia, and the Philippines as well as regional trainings in Central America, Southeast Asia, and the Middle East. The U.S. Government works collaboratively on many of these training programs with the private sector and with various international entities such as WIPO and INTERPOL.

- IPR protection is a main focus of the government-to-government technical assistance provided by the Commerce Department's Commercial Law Development Program (CLDP). CLDP programs address enforcement and adjudication of disputes, as well as IPR protection and its impact on the economy, IPR law compliance with the WTO TRIPS Agreement, IPR curricula in law schools, and public awareness campaigns. CLDP supports capacity building in innovation and technology transfer as well as in patent examination and copyright management in many countries worldwide. CLDP also works with the judiciary in various trading partners to improve the skills to effectively adjudicate IPR cases, and conducts interagency coordination programs to highlight the value of a whole-of-government approach to IPR protection and enforcement.

- The Department of Justice Criminal Division, using funding provided by and in cooperation with the Department of State, and in cooperation with other U.S. agencies, provides IPR enforcement training to foreign officials. Topics covered in these programs include investigating and prosecuting cases under intellectual property, economic/financial and organized crime statutes, combatting Internet piracy, intragovernmental and international cooperation and information sharing, obtaining and using electronic evidence; and the general importance of reducing counterfeiting and piracy. Major ongoing initiatives include multiple programs in Central and Eastern Europe, Asia, the Americas, and Africa.

- The U.S. Copyright Office, often in conjunction with various international visitor programs, hosts international visitors, including foreign government officials, to discuss and exchange information on the U.S. copyright system, its registration and recordation functions, and various international copyright issues. Staff also participates in a number of conferences in the United States and abroad to discuss current copyright issues and inform the public about the activities of the Copyright Office.

The United States reports annually to the WTO on its IPR capacity building efforts, including most recently in October 2013. (*See Technical Cooperation Activities: Information from Members – United States*, IP/C/W/594/Add.6).

ANNEX 3. THE WIPO PERFORMANCES AND PHONOGRAMS TREATY (WPPT) AND THE WIPO COPYRIGHT TREATY (WCT)

The United States continues to work with other governments, in consultation with U.S. copyright industries and other affected sectors, to develop strategies to address global IPR issues. In 1996, two new treaties were concluded at the World Intellectual Property Organization (WIPO): the WIPO Copyright Treaty (WCT) and the WIPO Performances and Phonograms Treaty (WPPT). Following their entry into force in 2002, these treaties have raised the standard of copyright protection around the world, particularly with regard to Internet-based delivery of copyrighted content. The WIPO Internet Treaties clarified certain exclusive rights and require signatories to provide adequate legal protection and effective legal remedies against the circumvention of certain technological measures as well as certain acts affecting rights management information. A growing number of trading partners are implementing the WIPO Internet Treaties to create a legal environment conducive to investment and growth in legitimate Internet-related businesses, services, and technologies.

As of April 2014, there are 92 contracting parties to the WPPT and 91 contracting parties to the WCT. Other trading partners have implemented key provisions of these treaties in their national laws without formally ratifying them. The United States urges other governments to ratify and implement the provisions of the WIPO Internet Treaties.

The following trading partner became party to the WCT between January 2013 and March 2014:

Algeria   Entry into Force: January 31, 2014

The following trading partner became party to the WPPT between January 2013 and March 2014:

Algeria   Entry into Force: January 31, 2014